Praise for
The Aging of Aquarius

If you want to make your retirement or "elderhood" the best part
of your life, read this book. Interspersing her own amazing story,
octogenarian Helen Wilkes points the way to purpose, passion,
and pleasure in later years. Wilkes has woven psychology,
philosophy, and poetry into a page-turner you will
not want to put down. I read it in one sitting.

— Dr.Roslyn Kunin, C.M., O.B.C., Roslyn Kunin and Associates, Inc.

In this inspiring work Helen Wilkes wastes no time raging against
the dying of the light, showing instead that the light of mind
and soul can shine ever more brightly even as our bodies grow old.
The Aging of Aquarius is both an intimate personal account and
a call to enlivenment and action for an entire generation.

— Gabor Maté M.D., author, *When The Body Says No: The Cost of Hidden Stress*

Whether you are contemplating retirement or well-established
in the business of living your senior years, this literary adventure
will nudge you to laugh at yourself, challenge yourself,
and discover both encouragement and inspiration.

— Sally Thorne, RN, PhD, FAAN, FCAHS, Professor, School of Nursing and
Associate Dean, Faculty of Applied Science, University of British Columbia

Wilkes' book stands out among a plethora of books on
this topic. It is beautifully written and avoids the usual clichés
and sentimental guff about the wonders of — to use that dreadful
phrase — the "Golden Years." It is not only a guide to living a good
and purposeful life for elders, but for people of any age.

— Roberta Rich, author, *The Midwife of Venice*, *The Harem Midwife*,
and *A Trial in Venice*

Reading *The Aging of Aquarius* touched me deeply, speaking to both mind and heart. Helen Wilkes brings core concepts alive with deeply moving stories and examples from the life of a woman who clearly understands and embodies the challenges and life-enhancing opportunities of growing into the fullness of true elderhood. In reading her beautiful book, I felt like I was personally engaging with a shining model of the kind of elder I aspire to grow into.

— Ron Pevny, Director, Center for Conscious Eldering
(www.centerforconsciouseldering.com)
and author, of *Conscious Living, Conscious Aging*

Beautifully written and rich in information, this book is a must-read, especially for Elders who have the richness of decades of experience and new found freedom to explore their lives with hope, curiosity, and positive thinking, leading to "Igniting Passion and Purpose as an Elder". A most important book for the ages!

— Ruth Neubauer, LCSW, Founder and Facilitator,
The Wisdom of Elderhood (elderhoodwisdom.org)

Don't wait until retirement to read this! Today is the day to walk the path of life-review with author Helen Wilkes. Let her simple prose draw you in. Through her personal stories, you'll learn the psychology, philosophy, and spirituality you need to confront your worries and find your purpose.

— Rabbi Dr. Laura Duhan-Kaplan, Director of Inter-Religious Studies,
Vancouver School of Theology

THE AGING OF
AQUARIUS

IGNITING PASSION & PURPOSE AS AN ELDER

HELEN WILKES

new society
PUBLISHERS

Cover design by Diane McIntosh.

Cover images: © iStock: senior woman – 98265490; watercolour texture (title) – 494763928

Printed in Canada. First printing September, 2018

Inquiries regarding requests to reprint all or part of *The Aging of Aquarius* should be addressed to New Society Publishers at the address below. To order directly from the publishers, please call toll-free (North America) 1-800-567-6772, or order online at www.newsociety.com

Any other inquiries can be directed by mail to:

New Society Publishers
P.O. Box 189, Gabriola Island, BC V0R 1X0, Canada
(250) 247-9737

LIBRARY AND ARCHIVES CANADA CATALOGUING IN PUBLICATION

Waldstein Wilkes, Helen, 1936-, author
    The aging of Aquarius : igniting passion & purpose as an elder / Helen Wilkes.

Includes index.
Issued in print and electronic formats.
ISBN 978-0-86571-894-4 (softcover).--ISBN 978-1-55092-687-3 (PDF).--ISBN 978-1-77142-283-3 (EPUB)

    1. Retirement--Planning. 2. Retirement--Psychological aspects. 3. Retirees--Psychology. 4. Retirees--Recreation. I. Title. II. Title: Igniting passion and purpose as an elder.

HQ1062.W54 2018   646.7'9   C2018-902846-7
                                         C2018-902847-5

Funded by the Government of Canada | Financé par le gouvernement du Canada

New Society Publishers' mission is to publish books that contribute in fundamental ways to building an ecologically sustainable and just society, and to do so with the least possible impact on the environment, in a manner that models this vision.

Contents

Daring

Delving Deeper

Deeper Still

Preface

AS AN OCTOGENARIAN, I've known my share of struggles and yes, sometimes my joints ache. However, contrary to all expectations, I'm not seeking to regain my lost youth. Truth be told, this past year has been the greatest ever, and I'm eagerly anticipating the next decade of life.

It has not always been thus. Lest you think I was born with a silver spoon in my mouth or that I am one of those insufferably cheerful people, permit me to introduce myself.

I was born to humble shopkeepers of Jewish heritage in a small village in the Sudetenland, a German-speaking region that had become part of Czechoslovakia following the First World War. Our village fell to Hitler when I was still in diapers, and as a consequence, I have spent a lifetime with fear and negativity as my constant companions. We fled, then we fled again, until finally, by sheer fluke, we landed penniless on an Ontario farm so dilapidated that no Canadian would buy it. With the remaining ten dollars that now constituted their entire fortune, my parents bought a cow so sick that it was dead the next morning. They learned to treasure the half-rotted apples that a neighbor invited them to collect from under his tree. It was a steep learning curve, but somehow, they survived.

Our home on the farm was a gloomy place where a wood stove barely heated the kitchen, and conversation was minimal. Not only were my parents exhausted by unaccustomed farm work, they were haunted by thoughts of what was happening to brothers, sisters, and parents, all trapped in the Nazi net. Rumors of extermination camps circulated throughout the war years, and at our table, anxiety hovered like an unwanted guest at every meal.

Others may have happy memories of school. My memories are of peers who mocked my halting, accented English, and who made barfing noises whenever I opened my lunchbox. Not until I was in Grade 6 did I have a friend, an equally lonely girl whose parents were also refugees. High school was an absolute nightmare of conflicting social pressures and personal isolation. The parents of my classmates forbade their sons to date me and encouraged their daughters to join a sorority that excluded me because I was Jewish.

This was doubly hurtful because the only religious education I had received was at a nearby church where I collected pamphlets of a blond, blue-eyed Christ, and where I learned to sing "Jesus Loves Me."

Eventually, thanks to a four-year scholarship, I attended university, but it was hardly blue skies ahead for a woman in the pre-feminist era. Although I had been one of only two people at my university who passed the grueling foreign-service entry exam in 1957, a government official informed me that Canada had never trained a female diplomat and had no intention of taking on a twenty-year-old girl who would only get married and waste her training.

After more years of study and earning a PhD, I did indeed get married, but it was not all "happily ever after." Marriage included putting my husband through grad school, but because he never finished his dissertation, his options were limited. The resulting stress in addition to other factors led to divorce when my children were respectively three and four years old.

Now, as I watch increasing numbers of friends lose a spouse, I think back to those bitterly unhappy days when I felt like the lonely unicorn, standing off to the side as, two by two, every creature clambered aboard Noah's ark. Divorce at the time was still so shameful that it took my mother several years to accept what she and her friends labeled as my "failure as a woman." For a long time, I simply stayed at home rather than enter a roomful of couples. Recovery was not easy. Recovery is never easy, and yet, in time, small steps become possible.

Awareness of the possible has given rise to this book. If, despite a childhood in the shadow of the Holocaust, and if, despite a lifetime of experiencing myself as an outsider with little sense of self-worth, I have found cause to hold my head high and to face the future with optimism in my retirement years, there is reason for others to hope.

Age certainly brings its share of pain and physical trauma. I fully recall the acute pain as well as the depressive effect of hearing that I was suffering from "degenerative disc disease." Still, after a bout of back surgery, I started going to the gym three times a week, activating sweat glands and stretching muscles I never knew existed. Now I see to what extent we owe it to ourselves to take good care of the body we have been given. It is only by doing so that we can maintain our strength to enjoy life while engaging in purposeful action.

Age also brings other losses, a reality from which there is no escape. Even the golden handshake is often accompanied by sadness at saying farewell to respected colleagues likely to soon forget their promises of staying in touch. Some who leave the workforce fear that retirement marks the beginning of a long slide into meaninglessness, unproductivity, and uselessness.

That has not been the case for most of my cohorts. We are a new generation, those of us who have had the good fortune not to be felled prematurely by accident or disease. Thanks to regular physical exercise, balanced nutrition, and the blind luck of good genes, for us, the years ahead multiply exponentially. Beyond that, medical progress holds the promise of time that once lay beyond everyone's reach. Many of us will now spend fully one third of our life in retirement.

I retired over twenty years ago. To my great surprise, these years have been by far the richest and happiest of my life. They have provided me with the opportunity to grow and to do, to wonder and to appreciate, to see new horizons everywhere. Whatever my initial misgivings about retirement, I have experienced it as a step forward into the realm of new possibilities.

I am far from alone in experiencing retirement as a gift. Around me, I see other seniors who have discovered how richly rewarding every hour of every day can become. Some of that may stem from an end to the distractions and demands of our middle years. I enjoy my grandchildren in ways that were not possible when my own daughters were their age. Beyond that, however, there is a vibrancy and an excitement that animates many older adults. I hear it in the voices of my contemporaries as they describe what they have just seen or heard, and what they have recently read or done. Their joy often has little connection to the life of idle self-indulgence that they had expected to lead in retirement. More often than not, their excitement arises from the contribution that they are making in the present, or from the impact they hope to have upon the future. Far from thinking that their best years have passed, they see how vital it is to maximize each day while making a meaningful contribution to the world of tomorrow.

They are living proof that aging is accompanied by a powerful urge to make a difference. Regardless of how greatly seniors may treasure their trophies and career accomplishments, regardless of how much they love and value their offspring, the past is not enough. They have a vision of doing more. Here's how Theodore Roszack describes this new vision:

> Boomers who will usher us into senior dominance are the best-educated, most socially conscientious, most politically savvy older generation the world has ever seen. ... Given sufficient awareness and inspiration, I believe that generation will want to do good things with the power that history has unexpectedly thrust upon it in its senior years.[i]

Maggie Kuhn, founder of the Grey Panthers, saw our situation thus:

> We are the elders, the experienced ones, ... responsible for the survival of our society. We are not wrinkled babies, succumbing to trivial, purposeless waste of our years and out time. We are a new breed of old people.[ii]

Mark Nepo expresses a related thought:

> The closer we get to light, the more fully we are lighted.
> The closer we get to truth and beauty, the more truthful
> and beautiful we become. In the same way, the closer we
> get to that sacred meadow called death, the more and
> more alive we grow.[iii]

Many of the seniors in my world bear out that sense of being lighted from within. They do not allow lack of imagination to limit their reality. At some level, they recognize that the failure to imagine that which does not yet exist leads to a life remembered, instead of to a life centered upon today and tomorrow. These seniors are deeply engaged in a range of meaningful, future-oriented activities. As a result, they exude energy and a breadth of vision that often exceeds what was possible during their "working" years.

Some are avid supporters of the arts; others are endeavoring to protect the environment. Some are passionate advocates for the dispossessed; others fund-raise or contribute hands-on work to bolster human health and welfare. One friend regularly visits prison inmates, while another collects unsold bread to deliver to soup kitchens that remain an unfortunate necessity for the mentally ill and homeless of our city. A third friend raises thousands of dollars for an African foundation by selling the products of her creative hands at bazaars and over the internet. Even in their nineties, some friends are freely reaching out to do their share.

All such activities are clearly aimed at alleviating suffering and at somehow leaving this world in better shape as a result of our having existed. They are proof positive of a tendency that philosophers of science are now calling "our god capacity."

> Science is making possible our broadest understanding of
> good and evil: the good is actions and systems that further
> the survival and continuing evolution of intelligent life;

the bad is what threatens it. But defining the good doesn't necessarily make it happen; we all know that science has also enabled terrible things on enormous scales. We need our god-capacity to generate the spiritual power — the motivation, trust, and faith in each other — to bring good about.[iv]

A number of scientists now claim that morality predates all current religions. They back up their claims with increasing evidence that morality is neither the product of parental teaching nor of formal education. They see the altruism so evident among seniors as a biological imperative not just for humans, but for all organisms. They claim that morality is part and parcel of our evolutionary inheritance, and that we would not have survived had cooperation and sharing not been built into our nature.[v] Instead of seeing selfishness as central to human behavior, they insist that compassion is a "hardwired response that we fine-tune and elaborate on in the course of our lives."[vi]

The elders who cross my path point toward just such fine-tuning. They are flexing their empathy muscles and learning to recognize the inherent value of others. Of course, I must acknowledge that they are also a privileged group. They are not among the homeless, the poverty-stricken, the mentally ill, or the addicted. Instead, they have acquired skills that allow them to work actively toward bringing about a better world. The most frequent complaint I hear is that twenty-four hours are not nearly enough to accomplish all that needs to be done in a day. They are proof positive that aging is a time to soar on a current of hope in human goodness.

—◦◦◦—

A few words of explanation.

1. Terminology:

Because there are no words free of individually or culturally assigned meaning, I have struggled to find suitable terminology for people "of a certain age." For anyone except a child to call someone "an old man" or "an old woman" is considered rude and offensive. To say that someone is "elderly" is gentler, but the word inevitably conjures up an image of frailty and weakness. Similarly, the word "senior" carries a whiff of British classism, inherited money, and masculine authority. It was primarily upper-class men who named their sons "William Johnson Jr." and expected deference as "William Johnson Sr."

I considered the word "oldster" because it reminds me of Nancy Drew's blue roadster, the dream car imprinted upon my imagination by the first book I ever read. Because cars are things that travel along unexplored roads, they symbolize the very opposite of the inertia, passivity, and jaded lassitude that initially, I feared would be the inescapable post-retirement reality. Nancy Drew's roadster appealed greatly because it was a convertible, open to the skies above, and open to the road ahead. Just the image I wanted as a symbol of life in the later years — a time to let the wind blow through our hair, clearing out the cobwebs and making room for new learning, awareness, and discovery. Alas, as the internet informs me, the word "oldster" is already fraught with attitude and with meanings quite unsuitable for my purposes.

That left me with the word "elder" which also carries varying connotations, especially when we look at cultures where it is inseparable from a degree of respect that is a far cry from the North-American norm. In Canada, the word "elder" has an especially strong link to Indigenous culture and, to me, using it merely to convey oldness carries a whiff of cultural appropriation. Besides, I think the word "elder," even in English, conveys an element of wisdom that is markedly different from merely getting old. To my way of thinking, a broad range of people in every culture may have a few words of wisdom to offer, but age by itself is not enough. Age alone does not confer wisdom, and some old people never morph into elders.

The gap in our terminology became especially clear as I groped for a noun for the later stage of life. We speak of childhood, adulthood, and then... we stumble, mumble, and verbally fumble about, not knowing how to label a major category. Somewhat reluctantly, then, I have accepted the need to speak of "elderhood," of "elders," and also to use the word "seniors."

2. References:

No doubt, my frequent referencing of other authors will appear excessive to some readers. However, I felt it important to do as much research as possible on a topic so wide in its scope and so deep in its potential application. Besides, I do have an academic background, with the result that I have thoroughly enjoyed delving into the thoughts and discoveries of researchers from diverse fields of expertise. Wherever possible, I have tried to digest and to simplify their insights and conclusions for the reader, while still giving appropriate credit to those whose work has influenced my thinking.

3. Biographical elements:

I have woven many of my own thoughts and personal experiences into this book. In large measure, I have done so in response to others who have assured me that their concerns do not differ greatly from mine. It is not always easy to slip serious topics into casual conversation and, as a result, every senior at times feels disconnected and lonely. Over the last few years, it has helped me greatly to verbalize difficult questions connected to aging. In the process, I have discovered that I am far from alone in my doubts or in my growing certainties. I hope that by being honest about myself, I can help others to feel less isolated as they look to the future.

4. Activating and personalizing the possible:

Although this book is an outgrowth of my own life experience, the "Idea and Action" component is meant to trigger thoughts on activating your own untapped potential. The goal of my questions is to help you move toward a life that feels energizing and purposeful for you.

This goal may require spending more than just a few moments allowing your answers to surface. I suggest that you actually take pen and paper in hand, and that you return repeatedly to your answers, amending, altering, and even totally changing direction as your clarity evolves and takes shape.

For the final, "Deeper Still" section, I set aside my questions, having decided that thoughts connected to death and dying were simply too personal and too intrusive to impose upon a diverse group of intelligent readers. The chapters of that section are meant to move you to a deeper place of introspection, and to help you reach personal answers that bring you to a place of peace.

Despite so much that is difficult to articulate, I strongly believe that our society has not yet caught up with the new world of aging. As elders, we are members of a cohort that is rapidly moving toward a new horizon. Wrinkles do not render us brainless, nor do they strip us of the desire to matter. As we contemplate how best to live each day, we often search for a fresh perspective. I hope my words will provide such a perspective. Moreover, I hope my words will inspire you to think and act in ways that promote a sense of self-worth as you embark on the trip of a lifetime, the journey to elderhood.

5. Acknowledgments:

Sincere thanks to Pat Dobie whose editing skills and helpful suggestions turned a draft into a manuscript. Equally sincere thanks to Peter Colenbrander whose intelligent comments and critique compelled me to re-examine many assumptions, and to delve more deeply into the issues. I appreciate greatly the seasoned advice of Peter Milroy who helped me navigate the complexities of finding a publisher. I owe much to Rob West, to the artistic designers and to the tireless staff at New Society who transformed a manuscript into a print-worthy book.

Sincere thanks also to the many friends who helped make this book happen. Some of you lent a hand directly, but most of you inspired this book by your own trailblazing life as elders.

Above all, I extend deepest gratitude to my daughters Rima and Reda. They believed in me, and they refused to let my self-doubts interfere with the completion of *The Aging of Aquarius*.

Diving In

Stepping into the Void

*The fear of death follows from the fear of
life. A man who lives fully is prepared to
die at any time.*

— Mark Twain

G RAVESTONES HAVE ALWAYS FASCINATED ME. At home and
abroad, I often find myself studying inscriptions and picturing
the lives of those whose bones lie buried, and of the broken-hearted
who stood at graveside while the coffin was lowered. Thus, on a lazy
Sunday afternoon in a small town in Germany, I joined a group of
locals who were touring a cemetery under the guidance of an enthu-
siastic taphophile. His knowledge of epitaphs and his appreciation of
tombstone art brought forth unexpected secrets from the grave. He
led an informative and utterly captivating tour.

As an outsider, I noticed immediately that almost invariably,
carved in bold capital letters, German gravestones feature the occu-
pation of the deceased.

Among the numerous inscriptions I noted was the term *Meister*
(master), used to indicate craftsmanship and professional aptitude.
Here lay not just an ordinary mechanic, but a *Mechanikermeister*. There
lay not just a hairdresser, but a *Friseurmeisterin*, a skilled coiffeuse. One
man's name was engraved as Johann Schmidt, Herr *Türmuhrenfabrikant*,
and I chuckled to think of the English equivalent — John Smith, Mr.
Manufacturer of Door Hinges.

Most women buried in cemeteries are remembered principally as
spouses. Such was the lot of the *Garnisonsverwaltungsinspektorswitwe*,

widow of the inspector of garrison administration. Perhaps this was a step up from being *Spenglermeistersgattin*, wife of a master plumber, but these are hardly words to reflect female individuality or accomplishment.

To me, these gravestones stood as reminders not to judge individuals by their social position or profession, but rather by the acts through which they demonstrate their inner worth and set in motion their deepest values.

On one tombstone, I spotted the following inscription:

Keine Tat, Kein Wort, Kein Gedanke, Geht Verloren.
Alles Bleibt Und Trägt Früchte.

No act, no word, no thought is ever lost.
Everything endures and bears fruit.

I found it comforting to think that our every thought, word, and deed might live on after our death. However, when I asked our cemetery guide whether Germans see death as "The Great Equalizer," he shook his head. He stated firmly that "a man's [sic] achievements are his crowning glory," and that "beyond work, life is over."

I was reminded of the German cemetery when I recently heard a professor of botany referred to as "the world's leading tomato expert." Undoubtedly, there are farmers, producers, greengrocers, and consumers everywhere indebted to his research, but will Mr. Tomato go happily to his grave with this tribute carved upon his tombstone?

Not long ago, while describing a young couple to my daughter, I said: "You'd really like them because they both work at..." Instantly, she interrupted with a reminder that she does not choose her friends for their professional status. Her words filled me with shame as I remembered fighting with my own mother during my dating years. How I hated it when her first question always seemed to be *Wer ist er*? "Who is he?" meaning "What is his professional or economic status?" I thought she should first have asked *Wie ist er*? "How is he?" or "What is he like? What kind of person is he?"

Still, for many people, status and professional achievement have become inseparable from their identity. The link becomes especially apparent when we are on the cusp of retirement. As we look toward the future, it is only natural to ask "Who will I be when I am no longer doctor, lawyer, merchant, chief...? Why will I get up in the morning when work no longer shapes my life? What will I do with myself all day?"

Ironically, keeping busy is not the problem.

A plethora of choices awaits every retiree. Any middle-class home has endless projects capable of soaking up time and attention. There are belongings and papers that need sorting and disposal, especially if downsizing looms on the horizon. There are gardens and garages that have been neglected, as well as kitchens, bathrooms, and furnishings that have not been upgraded. All too often, however, such projects only remind us of all the material possessions we have amassed, none of which brought the satisfaction promised by their advertisers.

Or we can stay busy "having fun." Many seniors now carry devices that allow instant access to their poison or passion of choice. For some, it is the latest news, stock report, or sports score. For others, it is food, fashion, or the lives of the rich and famous. Still others prefer games like bridge, poker, scrabble, solitaire, or one of a host of interactive, virtual reality activities. Just a few clicks and you are in the game, alone or with players who may be on the other side of the globe. And if you live in a city, you can experience your fun as spectator or participant at any number of venues.

Finding activities that bring a measure of inner satisfaction can be a far greater challenge. This is the key reason so many people express dread as the magic moment of retirement approaches. Suddenly, a deep fear replaces the dreams of leisure they harbored through every work-related setback. Moreover, it is natural sometimes to forget that images of "the good life" have been shaped by skillful promoters and effective advertising: "Relax with drink in hand under a palm tree, or perhaps on a deck chair aboard a cruise ship." And yet, those who have had such opportunities have often found boredom quickly setting in. For a while, that restlessness may vanish in a book or in another sleep-inducing drink, but sooner rather than later, people start searching for something to do or somewhere to go.

Nietzsche had already figured this out in 1886, at least as it concerned those of British stock:

> Industrious races find it a great hardship to be idle: it was a master stroke of ENGLISH instinct to hallow and begloom Sunday to such an extent that the Englishman unconsciously hankers for his week — and work-day — again.[1]

However, an ocean of difference separates "keeping busy" from feeling useful. For most of our adult lives, our work, along with family responsibilities, our work has defined us and given us a sense of coherence. When we teeter on the cusp of retirement, we know who we are within our professional world. Except for the increasingly rare, lifelong stay-at-home mom, work is in large measure the outward expression of our inner being.

As Ray Robertson points out, few things in life match the satisfaction of meaningful work:

> If one is fortunate enough to find one's occupational calling, there is a satisfaction ... so profound that it can't be achieved in any other fashion — or none that I've ever known. When I'm working — deeply, single-mindedly working — the only word that approximates the experience is absorbed.[2]

Few who have found this ideal marriage of inner qualities and external opportunities actively embrace retirement. For such people, retirement is a major transition that constitutes an existential turning point.

Nonetheless, the transition can and should be made. Failing to do so means failing to activate all that lies dormant within us. It also means we will reach the end of our days without having asked a key question, one that will to allow us to die without regret: How will I make my life meaningful as I move from the known into the void?

The answers to such questions are as unique as the circumstances of every life. Sometimes, those circumstances are difficult indeed. A marriage may have broken down. A loved one may have died prematurely. The unthinkable may have come to pass.

Even for the more fortunate retiree, the answer to "Now what?" may require leaving his/her comfort zone. This inevitable reality was corroborated by the work of a team of university researchers led by A. Leung. They tested people by giving them problems to solve while seated inside a very large box. Identical problems were given to a control group who were not placed in a box. Thinking outside the box led to far greater creativity of thought.[3]

To step outside one's habitual box can be disorienting. It can feel like the whiteout that skiers experience when snow falls so heavily that perspective vanishes. This leaves them with no signposts to distinguish up from down. Their total confusion is similar to the panic experienced by new retirees who see only a dizzying array of choices ahead.

Psychotherapist Thomas Moore likens the process of finding purposeful activity to alchemy, a process that can only occur if we first take stock of all our failures and disappointments and painful memories. At the same time, Moore counsels that we are never too old to do something we might consider irrational. His own father began piano lessons at age ninety-four.[4]

We are all the sum total of our experiences, good and bad. Unless we are honest about who we are and how we got here, we are likely to stay stuck in the past.

The answer to "Now What?" may take a singular form, when we find an aspect of our being that has lain dormant for years. Or it may be multifaceted, as we discover within ourselves an entire bucketful of undeveloped talents. The bottom line, however, is that we feel most fulfilled when we stretch to accomplish something or to meet a challenge. A life free from all struggle is not the recipe for happiness promised by amusing "Happy Retirement" greeting cards.

Alas, there is no one-size-fits-all answer to "Now What?" Figuring out what to do with the rest of your life (in all probability, at least a third of your days will be spent post-retirement) takes time. David Niven hits the nail on the head in his creatively entitled book *It's Not About the Shark: How to Solve Unsolvable Problems*:

> Your best answer is not a pizza. It is not going to be delivered within thirty minutes. But it will come. And when it does, it will be ... even better than pizza.[5]

As a starting point, Niven suggests two approaches:

1. **Fail with joy.** Try something that probably won't work and something that definitely won't work. We want to be right so much that we desperately try to avoid failure, but there's learning to be had in failing.

2. **Do something out of order.** Mix up your routine. It can be as minor as putting your sandwich together backwards — put the jelly on first today and then the peanut butter. When researchers had people do mundane things out of order, there was an 18 percent jump in cognitive flexibility scores.[6]

Retirement can be frightening, or it can be an exhilarating prospect. We can choose to avoid whatever frightens us, or we can dive deeply in search of greater fulfillment. Harold Kushner expressed it thus:

> I am convinced that it is not the fear of death, of our lives ending, that haunts our sleep so much as the fear that our lives will not have mattered, that as far as the world is concerned, we might as well never have lived. What we

miss in our lives, no matter how much we have, is that sense of meaning.[7]

In Germany, those historical gravestones I visited bore professional titles as the apex of human achievement. To the modern observer, a cloud of sadness clings to these testimonials. They speak of lives circumscribed by employment. They may be etched in stone, but they are a denial of our current reality. For increasing numbers of elders in the twenty-first century, the post-retirement years are the most interesting, the most productive, and often the most meaningful years that we will spend on this earth.

—◦◦◦—

IDEA:

You are facing a move from work to a retirement-based life and identity.

For many people, status and professional achievement are inseparable from their identity. This link becomes especially apparent when we stand on the brink of retirement. We have spent years taking pride in our accomplishments. Just when we thought it would be time to rest, complicated questions rise to the surface. *What is the meaning of life? Of my life in particular? Haven't I done enough?* It all feels overwhelming.

Now what? is always the first question to demand answers.

ACTION:

1. Believe in yourself. You are much more than the profession or the accomplishments that constitute your past. Like diamonds, we all have facets that remained unpolished as we tended to the necessities of life.

2. Spend time getting to know yourself. Was your pre-retirement identity based on your profession? Your

family responsibilities? Your creativity? Your willingness to take risks? Your determination to overcome obstacles? Other roles, values, or traits? Can you think of ways in which you received positive attention for that identity?

3. Picture yourself at a social gathering where you know very few people. Imagine introducing yourself to others without talking about your pre-retirement identity. List all your interests, from apple-growing to zookeeping. What lies just beyond the specific interest? Do you want to grow apples in a flourishing garden that is your vision of Eden, or are you passionate about preserving old varieties and wild fruit trees? Which aspects of yourself would you like a new acquaintance to recognize? What will be your new points of connection to others?

4. Write down what excites you.

    Two things I want to do before I die _____

    Two things I want to do this year _____

    Two things I want to do this month _____

    Two things I plan to do this week _____

    Two things I plan to do today for myself, my family, or for my friends _____

    One thing I plan to do today for my broader community, or for the world _____.

Facing Emptiness

In all our searching, the only thing we've
found that makes the emptiness bearable
is each other.

— Carl Sagan

WELL BEFORE THE ENLIGHTENMENT and the Age of Reason, the renowned mathematician Blaise Pascal pointed out that humans suffer greatly from a sense of inner emptiness.

> Nothing is as intolerable for people than being in a state of complete rest, without passions, without occupation, without diversion, without effort. That is when they feel their nullity, their inner loneliness, their inadequacy, their state of dependency, powerlessness, and emptiness.[8]

Many people compensate by keeping busy. During our working years, and especially if we are simultaneously raising a family, this is rarely a problem. When we become empty nesters, and in particular when we retire, Pascal's sense of inner emptiness hits us hard. Psychologist Mihaly Csikszentmihalyi writes that "most people who work experience a more enjoyable state of mind on the job than at home ... Yet few people would willingly work more and have less free, leisure time."[9]

At a recent dinner party where few of the grey-haired guests knew one another, the hostess suggested that we introduce ourselves by speaking first of our pre-retirement work and then of what we would have done had circumstances been different. I could not help noticing that the men who had risen to the top of their professions spoke with pride of their achievements and expressed no desire to change anything.

Almost all the women, however, had dreamt of making a larger impact than had heretofore been possible. Some had already made an important contribution both on the home front and in the wider world, yet they clearly yearned to develop skills that still lay dormant after a lifetime of endeavor. In part, this may be laid at the feet of parents who favored sons over daughters. In part, it may also be the fault of teachers who steered girls into coursework and careers that stretched neither mind nor imagination. I recall my own recoil when presented with the "opportunity" to learn shorthand and typing. Even then, I was appalled at the prospect of a lifetime spent copying down and neatly reproducing on paper the spoken words of a male superior.

I suspect that Csikszentmihalyi's contention that "few people would willingly work more and have less free, leisure time" derives its logic (in part) from its assumption of ingrained class-based thinking that construes work as an activity to be avoided. Despite not having been born "upper crust," we attach a measure of negativity to the very word "work." We may well admire ancestors for their struggles, but we feel entitled not to wear our fingers to the bone. We even label certain kinds of work "menial," and wherever possible, we delegate such tasks to new immigrants. We also distinguish between those who labor and those who "have" careers or professions, a parallel to "having" possessions and riches.

According to Csikszentmihalyi, there is an evolutionary explanation for our ambivalence about work. "If we could be contented just sitting by ourselves and thinking pleasant thoughts, who would be out chasing the saber-toothed tiger?"[10]

At every age, we need to be engaged. Life seems most worth living when we are deeply involved in activities that both absorb us and reward us with a sense of meaning. A close friend blossomed after retirement. Almost instantly, she volunteered with two organizations that required longer hours of service than her years of paid employment. Yet despite the long hours, she thrived. She worked gladly because it made her feel good about herself.

Passive entertainment often absorbs us, but only through our personal contribution do we glimpse a sense of meaning. I say "glimpse" in homage to scientists and researchers who study everything from black holes to cancer and may never discover The Answer. Still, they strive, and sometimes, ever so slowly, they move knowledge forward. It is the same for those who fight poverty or injustice in its myriad forms. No individual is likely to solve all these problems alone, yet by working collectively, people do move things forward — even if only a millimeter at a time.

As we move into the retirement years, the "wisdom years" that stretch ahead, it seems increasingly unsatisfying and even distasteful to be seeking little more than our own comfort and amusement. In an idle moment, I once penned this ditty:

> There once was a woman who'd worn many shoes
> She'd raised quite a flock, and at work she'd paid dues,
> She rewarded herself with cosmetics and clothes
> Her dreams having shrunk to the tip of her nose.
>
> The great gift of life she blew at the end
> Ignoring wide paths that lay 'round the bend.
> Not past it we stand, nor over the hill
> But itching to see what waits for us still.
>
> To reach and extend is everyone's need
> To quit without trying, to sadness will lead.
> So into the void let's leap once again
> It's not time to stop at three score and ten.

We may momentarily feel great posting photos of ourselves in some exotic setting, but successful retirement is a major transition. It requires that we plan for more than those moments of exceptional pleasure. Having conducted studies of various cultures and worked with thousands of individuals, George and Sedena Cappannelli stress the need to transition inwardly in retirement:

> The first part of our journey is primarily outward bound. We move away from the womb and in search of our place and stance in the world .... The second half of life is about ... focusing on a different set of values. It is about turning inward .... It is about making peace with the Earth, making sense of our time here, our role, the legacy we will leave behind us.[11]

Not long ago, I visited a friend who was nearing death. For days, I had agonized over what to say. Finally, I simply blurted out my admiration for all that she had done. Despite her outward control, this made her tears flow. Almost her very last words to me were "Thank you, Helen, for assuring me that I have not frittered away my days, and that my life has been meaningful."

Her final words confirmed social philosopher Michael Gurian's claim that "to serve is our life-work even in our last days," that "there is no time in our lives when service is secondary," and that "feelings of taking ultimately do not complete us."[12]

We may not have the power to control the future, but as elders we can lead the way. We can envision ways to contribute to the well-being of our fellow creatures. We can be responsible to ourselves and to the universe by interspersing our occasional escapism with outreach that leads to new horizons and to broader perspectives.

As elders, we know that we will be measured not by what we took in this life, but what we gave. That is the legacy we secretly hope to leave behind. And yet, blinded by fears and insecurities, we sometimes reach only into the past rather than step into the unknown. Fear leads us to slam shut the door to our own possibilities.

> Afraid of the anxiety that attends self-knowledge, afraid of the possible demands of authentic life, we run away,

hiding in false selves, or smaller selves, avoiding the challenge of our true self. Like blind tightrope walkers, we hesitate to move into the unknown. We hold on to whatever is within grasp: a handle, a straw, a house, a marriage, an idea, an identity, a belief, a piece of chocolate.[13]

As we transition into retirement, it may be tempting to clutch at straws and to crawl away into our own past. However, the path toward an authentic life requires us to stop seeing change as a dreaded specter. Instead, we must welcome change as the doorway to challenge and to transformation. Only by embracing the ever-evolving future can we deepen our experience of the present moment while expanding our awareness of all that connects us to life.

—⟨∿∿⟩—

IDEA:

Many of us feel a sense of inner emptiness. When we fail to acknowledge the hole within us, we end up trying to fill it with all the wrong things. These include excess possessions, a constant busyness, and distractions of all sorts. None of these solve the problem. That inner emptiness revolves around a deep-seated human need to make our one, precious life meaningful.

ACTION:

1. Have you ever wondered why people feel the need to talk about how busy they are? Do you find yourself doing this? What it this about? Why do you feel the need to do this?

2. Go for a walk — or just sit quietly for a while, with no reading material or other distraction. No music, no radio, no TV or electronic device. Listen only to your thoughts. Write them down.

3. Take another look at the quote in this chapter from Gunn's *Journeys into Emptiness*. Linger, and let his words speak to you.

   Afraid of the anxiety that attends self-knowledge, afraid of the possible demands of authentic life, we run away, hiding in false selves, or smaller selves, avoiding the challenge of our true self. Like blind tightrope walkers, we hesitate to move into the unknown. We hold on to whatever is within grasp: a handle, a straw, a house, a marriage, an idea, an identity, a belief, a piece of chocolate.[14]

4. Have you been hiding in a false self? Write down the names of any voices from the past (or in the present) that are making you feel small, unworthy, and incapable of further growth.

The Better New Days

Nothing is more responsible for the good
old days than a bad memory.

— Franklin Pierce Adams

THE GOOD OLD DAYS? Nonsense! Too often, these exaggerated tales of happy childhoods are highly censored versions of reality. Romanticizing the past is fine as long as we don't forget the ways in which society has also made huge strides in the right direction. I'm glad my grandchildren are encouraged to think things through and to voice their opinions instead of being told that children should be seen but not heard.[15] I am glad that their teachers encourage them to develop their talents, skills, and interests rather than steer them into so-called male/female professions, as was the case in my youth. I'm glad that my grandchildren wear comfortable clothes that feel good on their skin and that they can swim all summer long without fear of catching polio. It is easy to complain, but in so many ways, life *has* become better.

This was brought home to me by recent headlines of a woman charged with aggravated assault for going after her stepson with a wooden spoon. All my mother's friends had large wooden spoons in the kitchen. I never saw these spoons used for any other purpose than to threaten children (boys in particular) that they would soon "get it" again. I'm glad that society now frowns upon the process of degrading another human being. Personally, I know of no grandparent who would complacently stand by while corporal punishment is inflicted on a grandchild.

Does this mean that all grandparents are wise? Recently, I asked a group of retired friends whether they felt any wiser than before. Some looked puzzled, as if the thought of "wisdom" had never crossed their minds. Several men quipped that if you think you're wise, it's sure proof that you're not. In the end, the group concluded that many people simply spout whatever "truisms" they learned in their youth, and that far from getting wiser, people simply become more opinionated and inflexible in their views. "People have to have something to hang on to," they said, "irrespective of whether it is true or false, wise or foolish."

For me, finding *purpose* has become a goal more feasible than finding "wisdom." Wisdom is such an elusive concept that I fear thinking myself wise when I am merely opinionated. Purpose and meaning, on the other hand, are the very lifeblood that runs through my veins. They summon me from my slumbers each morning, and they accompany me as I drift back to sleep at day's end. They are pivotal to my daily activities and to the societal concerns that draw me towards action. Without them, I would feel trapped and ineffectual.

Here's how an experienced physician describes purpose:

> Purpose energizes. Purpose motivates. Purpose focuses. Purpose structures and fills a person's day.... Purpose is key to a vibrant, fulfilling, and empowering last one-third of life. Having purpose ... is one of the most important determinants of mental, social, spiritual, and physical well-being in later life. Purpose is special because you can have it no matter how old you are, no matter what your economic or social situation may be.[16]

Because they want to live purposefully, because they want to work alongside others in that endeavor, and because they want to remain active, some people postpone retirement, sometimes indefinitely. These words by Bill Gates Sr. struck me as relevant to many seniors who are reluctant to retire:

> People often ask me why — at the age of eighty-three —
> I still rise early every morning and drive to an office to
> work. I usually respond: I like working. I like the challenge
> of having to make decisions where there's always a risk
> of failing. I find that exhilarating. ... I'm much better off
> doing what I'm doing than I would be sitting on a beach.[17]

Bill Gates Sr. may well have choices not available to everyone. Some seniors have no choice. Others find their circumstances similar to those of Oliver von Bodenstein, the clever sleuth invented by Nele Neuhaus.

> On the drive home, he thought about his retirement. He
> would never again have to jump out of bed in the mid-
> dle of the night or ... worry about lack of personnel, tiffs
> among ... colleagues, ... regulations, restrictions, and
> tedious paperwork.... Would he miss ... the ... hunt, the
> feeling of doing something important and good, and the
> satisfaction of working together with his team? What
> sense of accomplishment would he have [if]...?[18]

For me too, leaving professional life triggered an existential crisis unrelieved by the financial planning session offered by my employer. I was much more concerned about personal issues. Who would I be once I'd lost the respect and admiration of the waves of students whose eager faces had greeted me for almost forty years on the morning after Labor Day? Who would replace the camaraderie of colleagues with whom I'd spent more hours in conversation than with my own family? Would I ever again want to set my alarm to start a project?

Today, I can hardly believe that I feared taking the next step. Retirement has not only brought me a new life, it has shaped a new me. That new person is willing and often eager to speak out, to face new challenges, to explore difference, and to seek out adventure physically, mentally, and spiritually.

I started by taking on a physical challenge. Shortly after I retired, two wise and supportive friends invited me to join them on a kayaking trip in the jungles of Belize. I pictured a living nightmare, with vines twisting along branches writhing with snakes and tarantulas. Even more frightening was the prospect of having to roll a kayak to qualify for daily expeditions into the trackless deep.

My aquaphobia may have begun with a perilous crossing of the North Atlantic when I was barely a toddler. I'm told I roamed the ship, lonely and abandoned, while my parents lay retching below deck, too seasick to leave their bunks. My fear of drowning was certainly exacerbated by the cruelty of children at the first summer camp I attended. Seeing that I was not a great swimmer, my campmates made a game of pushing my head under water each time I groped for a handhold. Eventually I reached the rocky shore of the lake, where I lay vomiting, exhausted, and deeply afraid.

And here I was in Belize, in my sixties, learning to roll a kayak and then to snorkel, opening myself up to underwater beauty beyond imagining. Tropical fish brushed my skin as I floated over a reef exploding with exotic shapes. Kayaking enabled me to visit uninhabited islands where lush greenery hosted colorful birds, animals, and a kaleidoscope of beautiful butterflies and insects.

The trip culminated in my ultimate bodily challenge, overcoming what is called cleithrophobia, the intense fear of being trapped underground, especially in a mine or cave. I have no idea where or when this phobia took root, but even in Disneyland, where I once accompanied my children on toy boats that passed through a miniature mine, I was frozen with fear. In Belize, we walked for an hour along a jungle path before swimming across a small river to the entrance of an unexcavated cave, where we were given a headlamp. In single file, we followed a guide into utter darkness.

The guide led us along what could hardly be called a track. It was more like a series of footholds over uneven terrain along which we groped our way, one hand always clinging to the rock wall for security.

Sometimes, the footholds were widely spaced and at varying heights, which meant using every bit of quadriceps strength to thrust ourselves forward. At other times, we had to worm our way through narrow gaps on our bellies, following only the reassuring voice of our guide. Had it been possible, I would have turned back, but having begun, there was no choice but to continue.

And suddenly, we reached a voluminous cavern. Here, miles underground, an ancient people had made blood sacrifices to nameless gods. Huge urns stood like silent sentinels in the faint glow of our headlamps. We too stood silent, absolute awe having stifled all speech. Still silent, we slowly followed our guide back to the light, to warm air, and to the now welcoming jungle path.

That narrow passageway which opened out into a vast cavern has become my guiding metaphor for the early stages of retirement. A small opening leading to unexpected treasure. A sliver of light in the darkness where our own inner treasure lies unseen and undiscovered. Until..., until we have the courage to crawl forward. Until we reach into the dark recesses of our own mind and find the riches within.

Had I yielded to fear, I would have missed out on a transformative trip. Travel is indeed both a window and a mirror. The window provides a new view of the world and its inhabitants, but the mirror enables us to see ourselves in a different light. Overcoming bodily fear brought me the necessary courage to tackle other fears. It helped me to greet retirement as an opportunity to make new discoveries. One of my favorite poets, Rainer Maria Rilke, said it best:

> Out of the darkest moments of my life, awareness arises
> that I have space within for a second, endlessly expansive
> life[19]

Rather than yield to nostalgia for "the good old days," rather than hanker for a romanticized past, rolling my mental kayak taught me to greet retirement as an opportunity for discovery.

IDEA:

> The good old days were not so good for a wide range of people. Those days included overt racism, sexism, ageism, homophobia, and physical brutality. While these have not disappeared, there is a greater awareness of what they are and that we should do everything in our power to combat them. Retirement means that it's time to roll our mental kayak. It's time to move from hankering for a romanticized past (in which we were stunningly beautiful/handsome/desirable/clever/socially sought-after, etc.) to a time when we become strong in ways that really matter.

ACTION:

1. List the attitudes you once held that have changed over time.

2. List also any behaviors in which you participated through ignorance or because you were afraid to stand against what "everyone" was saying.

3. What fears prevent you from finding greater fulfillment? Does this Rilke quote resonate for you, as it did for me?

   Out of the darkest moments of my life, awareness arises that I have space within for a second, endlessly expansive life.

4. Try something new, keeping in mind this old saying about aging:

   If I start now, do you know how old I'll be by the time I learn to _____?

   Answer: *Same age as you'll be if you don't.*

The Unmapped Road

"Come to the edge," he said.
"We can't, we're afraid!" they responded.
"Come to the edge," he said.
"We can't, we will fall!" they responded.
"Come to the edge," he said.
And so they came.
And he pushed them.
And they flew.

— Christopher Logue[20]

IT IS A WARM SUMMER EVENING AS I WRITE THESE WORDS. I've just spent time in the garden, enjoying the greenery in the company of a friend who retired recently. Her husband is planning to retire next year. She describes herself as "unsettled, in limbo" because she has no idea where to put her considerable energy. It is a problem that she fears her less flexible husband will find even more unsettling.

As an aspect of their retirement planning, they are both asking questions, beginning with "Where will we live? What interests have we left unexplored? What skills did we fail to develop? Are there goals we both want to pursue? Or avenues that each of us must investigate and act upon separately?"

My response, as so often, was to reach for a book. On my shelves stood Joan Chittister's *Following the Path*, a book whose subtitle continues to inspire me: *The Search for a Life of Passion, Purpose, and Joy.* Before lending it to my friend, I inserted a bookmark at the following citation: "We are all on our way to somewhere, however undefined, however unconscious... but to where?"[21]

The question has no easy answer. Retirement and "Coming of Age" have certain commonalities. Both are major turning points that necessitate finding the courage to go within. At King Arthur's legendary court, young men seeking to become knights were expected to enter the forest at its darkest point and to blaze a new trail. To tread where others had ventured was proof of cowardice. In other traditions, the young man enters the wilderness alone in search of his particular totem or spirit guide.

The retiree must also enter the forest alone. It requires a measure of heroism, but the rewards are great. Some retirees grow so passionate about their new pursuits that these become a calling more intense than their original careers. I know an elder who has taken up bird photography with an ardor that defies belief. Always an avid hiker and outdoorsman, he has now completed numerous courses to master digital photography. His current plan is to travel the world to photograph every single bird species in existence.

Recently, I met a woman whose parents had been village peasants in a communist country. Although she loved classical music, it was beyond her reach. However, she was bright, she studied hard and, after several detours, she became a structural engineer. Canada welcomed her skills.

After retirement, her priority was to rent a violin. With trepidation, she approached a teacher who showed her the basics, including how to hold the instrument. Alas, her sixty-five-year-old body had other ideas. No way would her back allow her to stand up straight to practice for an hour, let alone with one arm extended at a 90 degree angle, her head twisted to the side, while her other arm moved the bow across the strings.

Fortunately, the teacher encouraged her to stand for only five minutes at a time. Gradually, she extended the time to ten minutes, and finally, to a full quarter hour a day. Next, the teacher steered her to a physical trainer whose guidance strengthened her upper body.

Today, she plays in an orchestra, creating the classical music she once dreamt of hearing. And no, it's not the Berlin Philharmonic, but trying to become The Best at anything in a world of 7.5 billion people spells defeat. Retirement is about doing your best, not about comparing yourself to others.

Besides, unlike this woman, some retirees find it hard to identify a single central interest. They elect to grow outward, stretching their limbs like a bush rather than reaching upward like a Lombardy poplar. My own growth pattern is clearly bushy. Since retirement, I have learned Italian for no reason beyond the fact that I have always loved the musicality of the language as well as the operatic masterpieces created by Italian composers. I have attended numerous lectures, participated in various discussion groups, and delved into countless topics thanks to the miracle of libraries. Books, ideas, and the people who are passionate about them, these have broadened my horizons. They have also spawned new degrees of awareness that I am still in the process of widening and deepening. Where I once would have berated myself for lack of focus, I now give thanks for the variety and range of my interests.

One non-credit course inspired me to shape my personal history into book form. Books on the Holocaust rarely become bestsellers but *Letters from the Lost* won two major awards and gave rise to new and unexpected opportunities for growth, including radio and TV interviews, and speaking engagements in three countries.

Particularly surprising and pleasurable has been the discovery that I love writing. Never during my "working" years had it occurred to me to take pen in hand, yet now, every day, I look forward to sitting down at the computer and taking one small thought to wherever it will lead.

Opening up to reveal so much of my life and my thoughts has not been easy, but it has given me inner peace along with the strength to move forward in a number of ways. Now, I proudly wear the hat bequeathed to me by my friend D'vorah, the hat on whose band she had written the words "Silence is Complicity." She was a brilliant scholar who, when stricken by a progressive neurological disease, continued to act and agitate for change, first from her wheelchair and, later, from the confines of her bed. She never ceased to radiate her energy outward, influencing and inspiring others as she had once done in the halls of academia and in public spaces across the land. I never asked if she had been inspired by Pastor Niemöller's memorable words, but it is hard to imagine that she was not:

> When the Nazis came for the communists,
> I remained silent;
> I was not a communist.
>
> When they locked up the social democrats,
> I remained silent;
> I was not a social democrat.
>
> When they came for the trade unionists,
> I did not speak out;
> I was not a trade unionist.
>
> When they came for the Jews,
> I remained silent;
> I wasn't a Jew.
>
> When they came for me,
> There was no one left to speak out.

As an elder, I cannot singlehandedly stop injustice and wrong-doing, but I can refrain from looking the other way. As my Latin teacher once taught, *Homo sum, humani nihil a me alienum puto*. I am a human being, and nothing that is human is alien to me. As she explained the Terence quote, it means that each of us must respond in some way to that which is happening to our fellow humans.

My friend Susan K. recently sent me this Talmudic reminder that I must not allow myself to feel overwhelmed:

> Do not be daunted
> By the enormity
> Of the world's grief

Do justly now
Love mercy now
Walk humbly now

You are not obligated
To complete the work
But neither are you free

To abandon it.

In retirement, there are many ways in which to step forward. Opportunities to speak out, a chance to be of service, these arrive daily on our doorstep. Although none of my actions will remedy the flaws in our social safety net, stepping up to the plate makes me feel better about myself. Besides, as one legendary old man said to the young runner who scoffed to see him bend stiffly to pick up a stranded starfish and throw it into the ocean, "No, I can't save every stranded starfish on the beach, but I saved that one."

Regardless of the condition of our joints, each of us can bend a little to save a starfish. I recently heard of a young woman with a severe form of vestibulocerebellar syndrome. Doctors recommended that she lie horizontally for the rest of her life. After an initial period of shock, she became a pioneer in outreach via Skype to bedridden sufferers everywhere, offering soulful support to those in distress.

For me, bending involved learning to speak publicly about issues that I had formerly considered private. I also pushed myself to ask people to donate their hard-earned cash toward an important cause. To my surprise, I discovered that it is not so difficult to organize a group willing to convert ideas into reality. So many elders emerged from nowhere to lend a hand. Together, they made a difference. Now, I still see them making regular contributions in diverse fields of endeavor. One by one, they are tossing those starfish back into the sea.

If you are already doing the one thing in the world that you love best, if all you have ever wanted to do is dig deeper into the goldmine of your existing world, by all means continue. You may be among the many elders whose best work was done in their later years. Artists such as Monet, Degas, Georgia O'Keefe, and even Rembrandt reached new artistic heights even as their eyes failed. Indeed, the beauty of their paintings may owe less to perfect eyesight than to greater insight.

If, however, your work is simply what you do and what you have always done, I encourage you to rethink retirement. Don't just consider the economic realities of your situation. Give thought also to whatever excites or outrages you. What are your deepest values? Your longings? How will you try to effect change? "Good life" diversions have their place, but feeling truly good about oneself requires active involvement in something more.

After a pioneering study that followed subjects over the course of sixty years, George Vaillant confidently stated that "Successful aging means giving to others joyously whenever one is able, receiving from others gratefully whenever one needs it, and being greedy enough to develop one's own self in between."[22]

Mature self-respect requires both introspection and an assessment of the myriad options that lie before us as we age. The world is filled with opportunities, and the only trick is to choose among them. I urge you to explore, to adapt, to trade in your old expertise and to try something new. In old age, as in youth, even the longest journey begins with a single step.

—⁓—

IDEA:

> Retirement and coming-of-age are major transitions. Both require the courage to go within. Alas, there is no GPS to guide us on this journey.

ACTION:

> 1. Ask yourself whether you have developed your own potential. Did you long to paint, but decide that art was no way to earn a living? Did you long to play an instrument but know you'd never get to Carnegie Hall?

2. Ask yourself whether you feel obliged to respond to whatever is happening to our fellow humans, or to some aspect of planet earth. If yes, to which small step could you commit today?

3. If feeling good about oneself really does require more than pleasure and self-centered pursuits, what active involvement attracts you?

4. Gather some friends to play the game of "If I could, I would..." Clarify what you would do if you knew you couldn't fail. Commit to one small step in that direction.

Detoxing

What Didn't Happen

I can't change the direction of the wind,
but I can adjust my sails to always reach
my destination.

— Jimmy Dean

SOMEHOW, I HAD EXPECTED MY LIFE TO END shortly after retirement. That was the pattern in my childhood. A next-door neighbor retired in the summer and chatted with me daily across the garden fence. In the fall, we visited him several times in hospital. By Christmas, he was dead. My own father never even made it to retirement.

If I did manage to reach eighty, I expected to be frail, stooped, and tottering unsteadily with a cane. Mentally, I imagined that whatever wisps of thought might remain would center totally on my needs. Only occasionally would I remember others as they receded ghost-like into the distance.

That has definitely not come to pass. Although this has not always been the case, my body now serves me remarkably well. Others may view eighty as "over the hill," but for me, life remains a daily miracle. Of course, I've had to relegate some activities to history. I used to be a sought-after tennis player until a physiotherapist advised that repetitive motions would destroy my back.

What little I've had to relinquish has been offset by all that I have gained in the last twenty years. Imperceptibly, ever so gradually, time has opened my mind, honed my perceptions, and greatly enriched my life. Cultural commentator David Brooks calls aging our second education, one where, instead of a predetermined curriculum, "the information comes indirectly, seeping through the cracks of the windowpanes, from under the floorboards, and through the vents of the mind."[1]

As we age, it is incumbent upon us to keep those vents open. Ultimately, this allows us to choose our goals and determine how we wish to live out our days. Nothing compels us to adhere to the religion or class or ethnic group that is our heritage — unless we choose that as the tree where we will build our final nest.

We are of course, shaped by our experiences, but I am not convinced that experience is necessarily the best teacher. Negative experiences have rendered some elders as distrustful as a dog kicked by its owner. Like that dog, they snarl and snap and cannot trust that some humans are kind. I have watched some elders lump all members of a group together on the basis of their experience with a single person. Indeed, far from leading to wisdom, such so-called "experience" often leads to racism and other deplorable "isms."

Certainly, we all have a core personality that is separate from the sum total of our experiences. A gregarious friend who loves being with people recently told me how she struggles to balance her needs with those of her dearly beloved who is a total introvert and finds being in the company of others a disagreeable chore he'd rather avoid.

Our core personality tends to remain consistent through much of life, and it underlies many of the choices we make. Some people always opt for the familiar, for the known, for what they consider "the tried and true." They may hesitate to depart from the comfortable, whether it be food or the community they have always known.

If you are reading this book, however, I suspect that you are, like me, among those who seek to know the fullness of life rather than the narrow world of comfort and sameness. You are in the company of others who seek new paths toward actualizing their dreams. Author Judith Viorst argues persuasively that change is not the exclusive prerogative of the young:

Although our present is shaped by our past, personality changes are possible, even unto the seventh, eighth, ninth decade. We are never a "finished product" — we refine and we rearrange and we revise. Normal development doesn't end .... We can change in old age because every stage of our life, including our last one, affords new opportunities for change.[2]

The renowned Jungian analyst James Hollis makes a similar argument. He claims that "history writes messages upon us and through us," but although we are our history, "yet we are also something more."[3]

In my case, it is only since retirement that I have fully individuated and become true to myself. During my early years and throughout most of my adult life, I sought ego reinforcement and the approval of others. Of course, I still care what others think, but it is no longer the prime driver of my existence. Rather than listen to the siren song of the ego, I now listen for the whisper of that elusive "something more" that defines my essence. As I listen, I become increasingly aware of both the complexities of the world within and the magnitude of the external world.

How can I be beyond eighty and feel more alive than at any other time of my life? And how can it be that I am not alone in this experience? Here's what Oliver Sacks wrote on the eve of his eightieth birthday:

> My father, who lived to ninety-four, often said that the eighties had to be one of the most enjoyable decades of life. He felt ... not a shrinking but an enlargement of mental life and perspective.... I do not think of old age as an ever grimmer time that one must somehow endure and make the best of ... but as a time of ... freedom ... from urgencies of earlier days, ... to explore ... and to bind the thoughts and feelings of a lifetime together.[4]

Here's what Michael Gurian's widowed father wrote after a series of falls in his eighties led him to opt for a retirement community:

> People say these retirement communities shrivel them up, but that's not what I'm feeling. I'm in a whole new phase of life. I'm doing a lot, I have a lot of new friends, I teach an adult education class online, and I have the three-times-a-day hilarious experience of people-watching in the dining room! ... I definitely feel a new freedom. I tell you, Mike, it never ends, this growing up stuff.[5]

So much is clearly a matter of attitude. Physician Atul Gawande has observed that a surprising surge of positive emotions is integral to aging. He writes:

> If Maslow's hierarchy was right, then ... you would expect people to grow unhappier as they age. But ... people reported more positive emotions as they aged. They became less prone to anxiety, depression, and anger. They experienced trials ... and more moments of poignancy. But overall, they found living to be a more emotionally satisfying and stable experience as time passed, even as old age narrowed the lives they led.[6]

Of course, eighty is not eighteen, and energy sometimes flags. The list of people in my life who are facing serious illness, who are coping with chronic pain, or who are dealing with dementia grows longer by the day. Accidents and disease take their toll, and death spares no one. In my current inbox are details of the upcoming funeral of a former playmate of my own children. All of us have only this day to treasure fully and to experience with certainty.

A pathologist friend reminds me that even in body, we are not the same as we were yesterday. Every human body has between fifty and seventy-five *trillion* cells, each with its own lifespan, and all except brain cells need to be continuously replaced. He sums it up thus: it is a law of the universe that everything must change — otherwise there can be no time.

Purposeful action can be a part of any age. I hate it when I hear the young toss off a disdainful "Whatever!" I'm inspired by stories like this one from my *machatonister*.[7]

> Dad was lonely and sad after my Mom died so he decided to sell his condo and move to a seniors' residence. After a few weeks though, he noticed that it was very quiet and subdued. Dad was never one to sit around and wait for the undertaker to show up, so he approached the activities director about shaking things up. Instead of well-meaning school choirs and music from the 40s, he arranged for a drumming circle and play writing. The drumming did cause complaints at first but people were soon all in for the chance to bang and make noise. The play workshop led to a monthly event, where everyone had a part in the presentation. Afternoon tea time became "Happy Hour" twice a week, with dancing and lots of fun. There were, of course, some people who clung to their chairs and refused to do more than wait for the dining room door to open, but Dad was mentally and physically active till the day he died.

If you are healthy, get out of your armchair and work up a sweat. No, a bit of gardening and routine housework won't suffice. The older you get, the more essential it is to exercise as vigorously as possible on a regular schedule. If your body is already showing signs of deterioration, do whatever you can to halt further decay.

And what about the mental and spiritual decay that will settle upon you in the blink of an eye unless you stimulate your brain with more than the daily crossword?

Age is no longer as Shakespeare described it: *sans teeth, sans eyes, sans taste, sans everything*.[8] This year, my dentist assured me there is no reason I should ever lose my teeth, and a laser surgeon improved my vision by zapping a cataract in seconds. To me, food still tastes good, and I struggle to limit consumption of favorite treats lest my weight balloon and my arteries clog up. I have no desire to hasten my end.

In the future, a number of my body parts may have to be artificially created or grown in a test-tube, but how amazing that all this is even a possibility! Never am I likely to forget the museum exhibit in Shanghai of a human ear grown on the back of a mouse. Today's scientists and thinkers predict that the creation of life forms ranging from engineered vegetation to body parts is about to eclipse in importance the manufacture of material goods. Some see the century ahead as a time when humans will focus primarily on reaching immortality through a war waged upon death itself.[9]

Do we want a future filled with people whose bodies continue to function but whose minds do not? A recent Nielson report indicates that the average American already watches over five hours of TV per day.[10] That figure rises to seven hours for those over sixty-five. Is this the sum of what we have become as human beings?

Surely, all of us need to do some serious assessment as we age, rather than thinking about standing on a corner, watching all the girls go by, as The Four Lads used to sing in the 1950s.

I believe strongly that we are born to experience many things, to learn many things, and to do many things at every age. There are so many ways to give back to the world in return for what we have received and what we continue to receive. Failing to do so is an act of self-indulgence and ingratitude second to none. And, as Immanuel Kant said so clearly, "Ingratitude is the essence of vileness."

What didn't end at retirement need not end at eighty or beyond. Since I retired, I've been privileged to experience so much that lay beyond my wildest dreams. None of my grandchildren had been born when I left work. Experiencing their birth, watching them grow into fine human beings, that alone is a gift I can never repay. So is watching my children and their friends reach new pinnacles in their growth, transforming steadily as adults whom I respect and admire. Experiencing nature in its incredible variety and complexity, experiencing music and art and literature, experiencing a night sky on a cloudless night, these are gifts I can never repay. Receiving from friends, being with friends whose very existence makes my heart swell, these, too, are gifts I cannot repay.

Opportunities to receive are everywhere. Last week, rather than shift about restlessly in a lengthy line-up at a coffee shop, I talked to the woman behind me. Almost instantly, she identified herself as an Anglican minister who had experienced a call from God. I paused for a moment, then blurted out that I envied her because God never seems to speak to me. She smiled and asked if I had ever thought that God might speak, not in a thunderous voice from on high, but rather in the gentler voice of my friends and family. Bingo! A ten-minute conversation that triggered a major shift in how I hear and receive the world.

Whether I believe my gifts are god-sent or whether I see them as originating in the kindness of others, whether I find beauty in nature or in the artistry of talented humans, whether I see purpose as reflected by scientific discovery or by inward growth, there is no question that I continue to receive on a daily basis.

And if I can still receive, then with all my heart, I also long to give. The world still needs me to be here, and to do the best I can. Is there any other way to live?

—◦◦◦—

IDEA:

> In 1881, when Otto von Bismarck came up with the radical concept of retirement, few workers lived beyond age seventy. Today's retirees may have upwards of forty years ahead. In order to feel engaged, productive, and purposeful, it is essential that retirees give as well as receive.

ACTION:

1. Maslow's hierarchy of needs (culminating in self-actualization — the instinctual human need to make the most of one's abilities) has gained broad acceptance. How will you strive to self-actualize as you age? Do you hope to activate your full personal potential? If so, how do you plan to make that happen?

2. If Atul Gawande is right in claiming that people reported more positive emotions as they aged,[11] what emotions do you think they reported? What are your sources of positive emotion?

3. List the ways in which you might build upon these sources to increase your flow of energy.

4. List the ways in which you are currently receiving. List the ways in which you are currently giving. Have you struck a good balance?

Digging Deep for the Unique

*It's not how old you are, it's how you
are old.*

— Jules Renard

GIVING UP, saying that life is over when we retire, claiming we've done our bit and that we don't need to do more — these are not options for those seeking to live life to its fullest. Michael Gurian insists that "even the debilitation of our bodies, inevitably a companion of aging, can feel liberating if we spend time digging deep into the self in order to decide what our second chances [at life] need to be."[12]

Such digging requires a measure of truthfulness that may not have been necessary or even desirable in our earlier years when "fitting in" was a primary goal. With the passage of time, I find that I am increasingly detaching from the cultural imperatives defined by others. Instead, I turn to books, events, and, above all, to people who can expand my world. I look back ruefully and almost pitifully at the person I was in high school, university, and even much later.

Back then, I sought to belong by shaping myself to the tastes and values of others. I listened faithfully to radio programs featuring "this week's Top Twenty tunes," not because I liked the music, but because everyone else in my age group seemed to love it. I memorized baseball stats not out of interest in professional sports, but because I sought common ground where I might attract the male of the species. Now, I rejoice in being myself. Aging is like crossing the stage at graduation, a moment I experienced as a flash of freedom. Gone was the need to submit what I had produced to the judgment of a superior who ranked me as A,B,C, or, worse yet, the F that declared I had not only failed an exam but that I was a human failure as well.

In other ways too, elderhood is a kind of graduation. When we move from the authority of supervisors and from the judgment of colleagues, when we step instead onto the springboard of retirement, a similar flash of freedom occurs. Joan Chittister captures perfectly that moment of transition:

> To fall prey to image-making dooms us to the loss of the true self. To be accepted, to be approved. We call the store-bought decisions we make our own ... Until we can't make them fit anymore. Until the part of us that is true cries out for liberation so loudly there is no possible way to ignore it. Then we either break our chains or break down under them.[13]

Chittister enabled me to see that I have spent a lifetime feeling negative about what makes me different. Slowly, that negativity has given way to recognition that although I am unexceptional, I am nonetheless unique, as is every other person. As e.e.cummings wrote:

> To be nobody but yourself in a world which is doing its best, night and day, to make you everybody else — means to fight the hardest battle which any human being can fight; and never stop fighting.[14]

As we age, we need not pretend to like whatever the neighbors like, or even whatever our children and grandchildren like. Instead, it is time to appreciate whatever makes each of us individual. Aging is when we celebrate our uniqueness and rejoice in being ourselves.

***

It is Monday as I sit at my computer, and the weekend is still very much with me.

Friday afternoon, I made my way to a book launch in celebration of the author Lillian Zimmerman. At age ninety-two, Lillian chose to title her book *Did You Just Call Me Old Lady?* Then it was off to a Kabbalat Shabbat with my Jewish community. This meant an evening of shared food, music, and social banter along with the opportunity to go within and to become more fully aware of all that life has brought and continues to bring.

Saturday meant a lovely, lazy start to the day — time for that second cup of coffee and a few more pages of a book that gave rise to thoughts and ideas that would not have sprung up spontaneously without this outside stimulation. Then it was off to a discussion on death, dying, and the afterlife, topics that we all too often push aside. I welcomed the opportunity to hear what others think, and the chance to reassess my own thoughts on the subject. To my surprise, far from undergoing a gloomy afternoon, I was swept along to discover that even death can give rise to humor during a lively exchange of ideas.

Saturday evening was spent celebrating the sixth birthday of my youngest granddaughter at a public swimming pool. The very walls seemed to echo with the shouts and laughter of all her classmates and their siblings and their parents. It was such fun to see everyone happily splashing about and working up an appetite for pizza, assorted nibbles, and, of course, plenty of birthday cake.

Early Sunday morning, a friend collected me for breakfast, a fundraiser at her church for a local school where children often arrive hungry. This proved to be such a simple yet soul-satisfying way to add a drop of goodness to the world while socializing with people of all ages.

Sunday afternoon meant carpooling with a different group of friends, this time to attend a World Religions Conference being hosted by a local Muslim community. We were treated to brief speeches by an imam, a bishop, a rabbi, a Sikh, and by a Hindu leader before listening to their responses to challenging questions from the audience. Because world peace and outreach among different faiths, ethnicities, and nationalities matter so greatly to me, I found the afternoon hugely uplifting. I hope the people who prepared the delicious ethnic foods and organized the event welcomed my presence as greatly as I appreciated being there.

As I reflect on my own weekend, I see how clearly some combination of my background and interests leads me to seek to heal the "us and them" gap. Perhaps it is because I felt so excluded in my youth and during most of my adult years that, now, I long to serve as a bridge to those who are still marginalized or discounted. I continue to hope that by fostering and welcoming difference, we can tip the scales towards a world of inclusivity.

Other elders are drawn to saving endangered species, or to helping orphans in Third World countries, or to any of 1,001 causes and needs. Whatever the cause, whatever the need, we must grasp opportunities for involvement. If we fail to do so, we risk losing a major part of all that we are destined to be. I often return to these lines of a ditty I made up many years ago to keep myself on track:

> We must grow and become the tree
> That from the first, we were meant to be.

Although I may long to be a mighty oak instead of a thorny rose, the universe takes no account of my wishes. What the universe provides is nutritious soil that allows me to put down roots and to grow.

Growth may be painful at times. We may seek to avoid it by shutting down or by trying to imitate others, but such options inevitably lead to failure. That failure has been immortalized in the tale of the foolish student who spent a lifetime trying to be like his guru. At the moment of death, God did not say "Why were you not more like the teacher whom you so greatly admired?" Instead, God asked, "Why were you not fully yourself? How did you use the tools I gave you to express your own best self?"

To my surprise, aging has brought me greater appreciation of others. It has also deepened my admiration for their courage in facing personal trials. Beyond that, aging has brought enhanced awareness of the value of my own life, warts and all. Instead of striving as I once did to become more like those whose traits I admired — this one's thoughtfulness, that one's ability to crack jokes — I now accept that my role is different, but no less important.

This was recently brought home to me by an invitation to play a game in which I was to imagine trading souls for a day with anyone of my choice. Everyone else at the table chose a great figure, from Mahatma Gandhi to Maya Angelou, from Mother Teresa to Martin Luther King. I froze. My indecision was not for lack of a long list of people whom I admire. I froze because, for the first time ever, I realized that I am me, and that I want to be me. True, I'd like to be a better me, one who keeps growing and learning and doing more for others. True, I'd also like to have a different lens through which to view the world more broadly. That, however, does not mean that I'm willing to relinquish my own soul, my own core of being, not even for twenty-four hours.

I opted out of the game. I thought of that decision recently when someone asked me if I'd want to join the colonization of Mars proposed by billionaire Elon Musk. The speed of my refusal astounded me. The very thought of cutting short this life, of never again seeing family and friends, of never smelling another rose or eating another peach left me cold. My life is here on earth, and it is inextricably connected to the lives of others.

In my eighties, I remain astonished that I value my own uniqueness. Not my specialness or my talents or my accomplishments, but my individuality. Some call that a soul, God-given; others call it a human being forged by the miracle of genetic coding plus existential experience.

Personal uniqueness need not involve rigid constancy or unchanging fidelity to past positions. Age is your time to treasure your gifts, to activate your own potential, and to discover your own unique value.

—◦∞◦—

IDEA:

The need to conform, the need for acceptance, these shape our youth and much of our adult life. Age allows us to individuate and to value our own uniqueness.

ACTION:

1. Have you begun the process of individuation? Reflect back through the decades. Write down the ways in which you have changed and the specific events that triggered each change.

2. Like e.e.cummings, do you experience the world as "doing its best to make you like everyone else"? How are you expressing your own uniqueness?

3. Which of your traits, attitudes, values, behaviors have you begun to appreciate? Are you still a square peg trying to fit into a round hole? Which aspects of your own special shape do you cherish?

4. Gather a group of friends. Invite them to join you in a game of "If I could trade souls with anyone, living or dead, for twenty-four hours, I'd choose _____"

Throwing Open the Shutters

*Aging is not lost youth but a new stage
of opportunity and strength.*

— Betty Friedan

I USED TO ENVY SELF-ASSURED PEOPLE. As I floundered through life, they seemed so certain of their positions and perceptions. Now I see that often, they had merely closed down their options. I remember a classmate who threw her diploma into the air on the day we graduated from university, triumphantly shouting, "Yippee! Now I'll never have to read another book!" She wasn't joking. When I met her at the fifty-year reunion of our graduating class, I could not fail to notice how shallow and self-centered she had become.

As I age and gain in experience, I have begun to think of that classmate and others like her as people who live in houses without windows. They feel safe and they may be warm, but very little enters or leaves through the narrow doorway of their lives.

Recently, I visited a friend whose gradual dependency struck me as an almost voluntary shutting down. For years, her conversation focused on how things were in the old days, when she used to enjoy life. That was when she was admired by others as she made her entrance on the arm of her well-known husband. After he died, she looked increasingly to her children and grandchildren to fill the void. When they chose to pursue their own interests, she gave up.

This person, who once seemed so cultured, so open to humanity's artistic, musical, and intellectual gifts has spent years allowing little new to enter her world. Although her memory is excellent and she is as self-assured as ever, she clings to opinions rooted in a world that no longer exists. To me, her certainty smells as stale as last year's lavender.

I have watched with sadness as other friends engage in this voluntary shutting down. With nothing to lure her from her slumbers, Jeannie began to say "I don't do mornings." Then she began to say "I don't like to go out after dark." With outings increasingly limited to mid-afternoon at the senior's center, her mind gradually lost its sharpness. Her curiosity about the outside world faded along with her energy, and soon, the lively soul I had known shrivelled into a dusty shell I scarcely recognized. Another friend who rarely leaves his TV set recently phoned me at 3 p.m., saying (I'm not sure whether apologetically or proudly) that he had just had breakfast.

As we age, we need lots of windows in the walls that shelter us. Sometimes, this means leaving our "comfort zones" and becoming adventurous. Increasingly, I see wisdom not as a place of certainty, but as a process of staying open and responsive. Change is inevitable, and one measure of wisdom is surely the ability to stay open to new concepts. In the world of my youth, the very word "cisgender" was unknown, yet today, I am thankful for the awareness that it brings to our society and to each of us as individuals. I have learned that there are many old assumptions that I need to pitch along with possessions that clutter my closets but add no joy to life.

I fail to understand the fears of those who shy from everything unexpected. So often, something completely unplanned brightens my day. New opportunities, new encounters, new experiences along with new thoughts, freshly awakened feelings, and greater awareness. How could I turn my back on these for the illusion of safety? Ultimately, we are all vulnerable to a range of disasters for which there can be no preparation. My small earthquake kit with a few bottles of water and emergency supplies will be small comfort if the earth shakes and a building falls upon those I love.

Besides, aging is so utterly and wondrously different from the obligation-filled existence of my early adult years. Now, as six o'clock approaches, it no longer means "Oh my gosh, what'll I make for dinner?" Sometimes, I'll grab an apple and go watch a sunset. Sometimes, I'll grab cheese and crackers before heading to some interesting event that starts at 7 p.m.

Being free to choose our goals is a luxury few of us had during what I look back on as "the years of being responsible." In childhood, we were responsible to parents and teachers whom we tried to please as best we could. Then we became responsible to spouses and children and to the world of work. Finally, we completed the circle by becoming responsible for the care and comfort of aging parents. Now, we are free to choose goals and to make these our own in a whole new way. Seniors who choose to run a marathon approach the challenge with an inner-driven excitement that surprises seasoned trainers. Seniors who choose to paint or draw find themselves lost for hours, eyes and mind fully focused on a square of paper or canvas.

"Take that first step," I often command myself, "even if you are not certain where it will lead." Others seem to admire my ability to do that, whereas I cannot imagine the stultifying routines that some people follow in order to give structure to their life. A while ago, I went to New York because of a special event that drew me. People asked "Was it a tour? Who did you go with?" It had not occurred to me that I needed a sidekick in order to go to one of the most fascinating and varied cities in the world. The same happened a few years before when I was heading to Europe and found my best flight was via Amsterdam. Why would I go through a world class city that I had never visited and not stop to explore? I had a fabulous week of meeting interesting people, seeing unexpected sights, and experiencing heart-stopping moments of gazing at Rembrandts and other fabulous works of art. To make it even better, it was tulip season. I can't recall when I last felt so bathed in beauty.

Another of the surprising gifts of aging is the fact that I no longer feel the need to be with someone twenty-four seven. I am happy for my partnered friends for whom togetherness is an ongoing source of joy. However, I hope they have not surrendered the need to foster their own development. A while ago, I took my grandsons to a museum of paleontology. One of them gazed in wonderment at the skeleton suspended from the ceiling in the vast foyer. "Wow! Look at that giant Blue Whale!" he exclaimed. When I asked how he knew it was a Blue Whale rather than a Grey or an Orca, he looked at me rather scornfully and said: "Well, look at it! You can tell from its rib structure." Dearly as I love my grandson, I do not share his current passion for dinosaurs and the subsequent knowledge of skeletal structures that is the outgrowth of that passion. We often love people whose enthusiasms we do not share.

We are all uniquely individual in our interests and, sometimes, we need to withstand the forces that encourage conformity at the expense of creativity. Some people end up doing what "everyone else is doing" rather than follow their own dreams and visions. In retirement, it is by feeding our own curiosity that we individuate and grow strong, even if that is sometimes accompanied by a sense of loneliness. The sixties icon Janis Joplin, who was as isolated off stage as she was intensely bonded with others while performing, said shortly before her death that she was working on a tune called "I just made love to twenty-five thousand people, but I'm going home alone."[15]

As I become more open about sharing my thoughts with others, I find that I am far from alone. Other elders are stepping back from the world of endless acquisition to ask what really matters. They, too, are seeking ways to live accordingly. They do not always verbalize their questions, but everything that I've read indicates that "life review" becomes inescapable as the end approaches.

While some people will primarily remember their successes, my experience is that most often, when we are alone with our thoughts, we ask "How did I fail? Whom have I hurt or disappointed? How could I have done better? To whom do I owe an apology? To whom have I failed to express my appreciation? What must I do while there is still time?"

Some seniors see such questions as bearing only upon their family and their immediate social circle. For others, the question has broader implications. I remain convinced that almost all of us want our lives to have been a force for good. This longing may sound pretentious, even preposterous given that each of us is just one person with limited influence and insight. Still, that does not prevent us from having such longings.

I think often of the Emily Dickinson poem that I call "If."

> If I can stop one Heart from breaking
> I shall not live in vain
> If I can ease one Life the Aching
> Or cool one pain
> Or help one fainting Robin
> Unto his Nest again
> I shall not live in Vain[16]

While I seldom encounter fainting robins, I do find other opportunities to be useful. Like every elder, I long to do whatever I can. Of course, life imposes restrictions and places limits on what is possible. For some unfortunates, limitations are imposed at birth, through the unequal distribution of ability or through the lottery of inadequate parenting. For others, the limitations come later in life. Among the greatest restrictions, however, are those that are self-imposed.

Just yesterday I heard of a man born with no arms who loved music. Sitting on a chair raised above the keyboard, he has taught himself to play the piano with his toes. When asked about this extraordinary accomplishment, he shrugged and said "I can either hope to die soon, or I can live a challenging and fulfilled life."

I cannot help contrasting this man's attitude with that of my mother. She was only forty-eight when my father died. "I'm too old!" she exclaimed, when I urged her to learn to drive the car. "It's too late!" she protested, when I tried to sign her up for a course that would allow her to escape her dead-end job.

Like my mother, there are some who opt to keep the windows to life shuttered. They view change as a threat rather than as a challenge and an opportunity. They shy away from learning, from growing, and from adapting to new realities. With age, I am drawn to the image of life as a river, an image that requires us to be fluid and flowing rather than solid and stable like a house of bricks. Here's how cultural anthropologist Angeles Arrien explains it:

> Rivers are nature's teachers and exemplify flexibility, resilience, and perseverance, all qualities that are both necessary and available to us in our later years. To live "Like a river flows / Carried by the surprise / Of its own unfolding" is the supreme invitation of the second half of life.[17]

At some level, all of us are creatures of habit. Major adjustments to attitude, opinion, or lifestyle can be uncomfortable at any age. But how much is lost when we fail to step into the river? When we do not live up to our own potential? When we fail to contribute to the world all that our heart longs to give?

―〰〰―

IDEA:

> Among life's greatest restrictions are those that are self-imposed. Sometimes, old attitudes need to be pitched along with the clutter in our closets. Like a house in which old air is endlessly recycled, a mind that has no space for anything fresh is a place of staleness and a breeding ground for diseased thought.

ACTION:

1. List your favourite sayings and check their expiry date. Here are a few to get you started:

   a. *Never trust a stranger.* Maybe there's a difference between hearing these words as a child and abiding by them as a capable adult. Isn't it time you replaced it with the biblical admonition "Be kind to the stranger, for you were once strangers in Egypt."

b. *You can't teach an old dog new tricks.* Maybe that used to be true, but haven't the last few decades taught you anything? Maybe it's time to replace that old adage with words attributed to Sophia Loren: "There is a fountain of youth: it is your mind, your talents, the creativity you bring to your life and the lives of people you love. When you learn to tap this source, you will truly have defeated age."

c. *Ours not to reason why, ours but to do and die.* Maybe, instead of viewing Tennyson's words as a motto by which to live, as did the poor innocents of the Charge of the Light Brigade whom I was taught to admire, it is time to view the life of every young man as precious regardless of whether he was conscripted by Group A or by Group B.

Yes, ours *is* to reason why. Moreover, our task is to ask difficult questions for which there may be no simple answer. But that is our challenge, especially as elders who have seen so much of life. We know that simply obeying orders is not enough. That's why, ever since Nuremberg, we hold individuals responsible for their actions.

2. Are you the victim of self-imposed restrictions? Do you tell yourself: "I'm too old to_____"?

3. Are you an absolutist, telling yourself that if you can't reach the top of a mountain, there's no point in taking a long walk, let alone in climbing a hill? Do you forgo partial accomplishment because reaching the summit seems impossible?

4. Ask family and friends to tell you which sayings they've heard you cite. For each slogan or proverb, try to come up with an opposite perspective that might be more inspiring.

Fostering Well-Being

Health is infinite and expansive in mode and world; whereas disease is finite and reductive in mode, and endeavors to reduce the world to itself.

— Oliver Sacks, *Awakenings* (1973)

IN RETIREMENT, former US president Jimmy Carter asked the question "What is good health?" His answer extends far beyond the absence of physical illness: "More than being able-bodied, it involves self-regard, control over our own affairs, strong ties with other people, and a purpose in life."[18]

Carter's four criteria gave me pause as I examined each in turn. *Self-regard* is a concept I have found particularly problematic, having been raised to think of it as akin to self-centeredness and selfishness. Moreover, Carter has always struck me as a modest man, one I had expected to steer the reader more towards humility, a quality I had long perceived as much needed and constituting the very heart of wisdom, especially as we age. I thought of old age as the period when, like the one-term president, we begin to see our failures writ large and our self-worth diminished as our modest accomplishments are erased or surpassed by the innovations of a younger cohort.

Finding ways to keep our small successes in perspective is no easy task. Fortunately, it becomes easier with age. Perhaps this is due to the experience of no longer being in daily competition with others. Psychiatrist and author Kevin Solomons claims that we start life seeking to please mother. However, the techniques we use to win her approval are likely to fail as our circles widen. If our sense of self-worth merely shifts from mother to winning the approval of peers, we remain vulnerable to low self-esteem. As a result, we overvalue what we are not, and we undervalue what we are.[19]

Genuine self-regard is as far removed from extreme self-denigration as it is from self-aggrandizement. I think back to a recent conversation with a highly-regarded young woman whose work-related successes are blazing the trail to a new future. Nonetheless, she feels that does not measure up, that she is failing to climb fast enough up the career ladder, and that whenever "success" seems within her grasp, someone raises the bar. She feels that her entire existence is bound up in the perceptions of her colleagues and professional superiors.

I saw my younger self reflected in this woman's struggles. When our career trajectory is dependent on the high opinion of others, treading on toes becomes dangerous. Now I speak up where once I might have bitten my tongue. Age has provided me with a stronger self-regard that allows me to voice views that may differ from those commonly held. My friends joke that I am like the fabled child who exclaims: "But the emperor whose fine clothes you are admiring is buck naked!"

During the course of a recent radio interview, I heard the well-known environmentalist David Suzuki express his delight at turning eighty. He sees it as a time when he no longer needs to curry favor with granting agencies, a time to voice his opinion and to assume the mantle of elder. His words struck me as the very embodiment of self-regard, based not on egotism but on balanced self-assessment:

> I speak today as an elder... We can speak the truth from our hearts and if that offends anyone, that's their problem, not mine. And elders have something no other group in society has — we've lived an entire life. We've learned a lot and it's our responsibility to sift through our hard-won life lessons for those that are worth passing on to the coming generation.[20]

Can there be a similar balance that permits us to feel that we have *control over our own affairs*, the second of Carter's criteria for good health? When my car falters, I call a mechanic. When my taps leak, I call a plumber, and when the lights flicker, it's time for an electrician. I know that there are men — and increasing numbers of women — who haul out their toolboxes, but I am not among them. No one can do it all, and I see no shame in acknowledging that I cannot do what others take in their stride.

However, because we live in a society that stresses self-sufficiency, we tend to forget that we are all interdependent. In the last week alone, I have visited one friend who has opted for a care facility, and a second friend with serious health and mobility issues requiring daily house-calls by trained professionals. Needing help does not mean lack of control over our affairs. I am full of admiration for those who reach out for assistance. They are "in control" because they know their limitations, just as I acknowledge my own.

I have never understood what happens under the hood of my car or inside my washing machine, let alone what causes body parts to ache. Still, despite such huge gaps in self-sufficiency, I have been able to purchase a home, educate my children, earn a pension, and even set aside a little extra. What greater control over my own affairs could I possibly want?

Everyone requires a supportive team of experts to manage certain aspects of well-being. That is a process that will increase steadily in the years ahead. However, regardless of the nature of the help that may yet be needed, control over my own affairs continues to be a gift of aging.

Carter's third criterion, *strong ties with other people*, seems self-evident. Still, having no brothers or sisters, I am astounded to hear of families whose ties exist only through their birth certificates. I have a friend who has declared herself divorced from her abusive mother, her siblings, and her entire birth clan. Another friend hears occasionally from a brother whose lifestyle and values are now so distant from her own that they no longer share anything except the rapidly receding memory of their deceased parents. The sole contact between a third friend and his grandchildren takes the form of checks that he writes at Christmas, for which he receives a perfunctory text message of thanks in return.

All of us need close family connections. If these are not possible, we can replace them with intimate friendships or with wider community connections. I love the family of adopted adults and surrogate grandchildren who grace my table at holiday time. They compensate for the extended family of which I was stripped, and they bring me deep comfort.

Overlooked, sometimes, are extensions of our own family. For many seniors, the need for strong ties with others awakens interest in family history. For some, genealogy becomes almost a compulsion. Certainly, it is a tree of investigation that can bear nutritious fruit.

I have tasted some of that fruit by reaching out in search of the extended family I had known only in my infancy — the uncles, aunts, cousins, and grandparents whose absence had left a gaping hole in my life. Finding even partial traces of their reality has left me both rooted and enriched in ways I could not have foreseen.

Perhaps like trees, we struggle to stand straight and tall unless we have solid roots. People have pointed out that since my last trip to Germany, I have become a calmer person. I believe this has little to do with what the Germans did or did not do during the Second World War, and much to do with being at peace with myself. Once I had made sense of my parents' lives, once I had perceived my position as part of a greater whole, I experienced myself as connected to others in an entirely new way. Now, I encourage fellow retirees to develop strong roots by delving into their own family history.

Carter's final criterion, finding one's *purpose in life*, is undoubtedly the greatest challenge of all. Everyone finds purpose in a different way. Because there is no such thing as a run-of-the-mill human being, there can be no one-size-fits-all purpose. As Viktor Frankl has explained, generalizing about the meaning or purpose of life is akin to asking a chess master to reveal the best move in the world. There simply are no such moves that can be detached from their particular situation.

> One should not search for an abstract meaning of life. Everyone has his specific vocation or mission in life to carry out a concrete assignment which demands fulfillment. Therein he cannot be replaced, nor can his life be repeated. Thus, everyone's task is as unique as his specific opportunity to implement it.[21]

What is clear, however, is that we are unlikely to find purpose unless we seek it. Many people fail to find their purpose because they cannot face the intense soul-searching that inevitably follows.

I wrestle with life. I read books on philosophy and religion, on cosmology and quantum physics. Maybe that's not for you. Maybe you neither want nor need to delve into your life history. Again, we are all different.

Charles Schulz once drew a Peanuts cartoon in which Snoopy said: "My life has no purpose, no direction, no aim, no meaning, and yet I'm happy. I can't figure it out. What am I doing right?" Yet Schulz himself produced six daily strips and a Sunday edition for almost fifty years, drawing every one of his 17,897 Peanuts comic strips by himself. He is quoted as saying: "I would feel just terrible if I couldn't draw comic strips. I would feel very empty if I were not allowed to do this sort of thing."[22]

For some years, brain researchers have claimed that having a sense of purpose in life is related to longevity. Unlike our daily chores and mundane tasks, purpose involves the desire to make a difference in the world. Clearly, "People who have such a purpose believe that their lives are more meaningful and more satisfying. They are more resilient and motivated, and they have the drive to muddle through the good and the bad of life in order to accomplish their goals."[23]

Neuropsychologist Patricia Boyle and her colleagues at the Rush Medical Center discovered that participants who agreed with the following statements were likely to die sooner:

- I sometimes feel as if I've done all there is to do in life.

- I used to set goals for myself, but now that seems like a waste of time.
- My daily activities often seem trivial and unimportant to me.[24]

Unanimously, cognitive neuroscientists and neuropsychologists urge seniors to avoid the paths of stagnation and sameness. In describing himself in his 2005 book *The Wisdom Paradox*, Elkhonon Goldberg (born in 1946) affirms that decline is not a necessity:

> I am not more stupid … than I was thirty years ago. My mind is not dimmed; in some ways it may in fact be working better. And as psychological (and hopefully also real) protection against the effects of aging, I find myself constantly propelling myself into forward motion. A life too settled is no longer a life but an afterlife, and I want no part of it for myself.[25]

Science confirms that Jimmy Carter got it right. Good health is more than just the absence of illness. Indeed, good health may not be the same as optimal physical health. Increasingly, it becomes evident to me that my real health flows from strong ties that I've established with other people. It also flows from greater control over my own affairs than was possible during my working years. Most importantly, it flows from the gift of time that has allowed me to experience life as purposeful.

All these factors combine in a multitude of mysterious ways. Even more than my physical health, it is this well-being that I treasure. I hope that this well-being will be mine regardless of what may befall the body. Knees give out, backs ache, but what is priceless is feeling respect for the person I am in the process of becoming.

—⁓—

IDEA:

> "Good health is much more than merely the absence of physical illness. It includes self-regard, control over our own affairs, strong ties with other people, and a purpose in life."[26]

ACTION:

1. **Self-regard.** Many of us have learned the art of self-disparagement. Instead of berating yourself for ways in which you have disappointed others, or you failed to live up to your own expectations, or you actually made a mistake, try patting yourself on the back at least as often as you beat up on yourself. Surely you also have some admirable qualities! Next, picture yourself in a similar situation. Clarify how you will act, and how you will draw upon your strengths to effect a more positive outcome. Then, let it go.

2. **Control over our own affairs.** Many of us have exaggerated notions of our own self-sufficiency. North American culture stresses the need for independence at an early age. Self-sufficiency remains a hallmark of adult life, leading us to underestimate the degree of interdependency we all experience. When someone offers you a seat on the bus, or holds open a door, or helps in some way, why not see yourself as providing an opportunity for others to serve and to be helpful?

3. **Strong ties with other people.** Do you have strong family ties — as opposed to mere obligations? If so, you are fortunate. Enjoy! If your family is scattered far and wide, have you converted friends into family? Have you expressed the desire to be included at their table during the holidays, and do you include them in your own celebrations? If you *really* feel socially isolated, then ACT NOW!

   A study at the Cognitive Neurology and Alzheimer's Disease Center (CNADC) at Northwestern University Feinberg School of Medicine on SuperAgers — people 80 years of age and older who have cognitive

ability at least as good as people in their 50s or 60s —
reported having more satisfying, high-quality relationships compared to their cognitively average,
same-age peers.[27]

Researchers increasingly cite social isolation as a major
health risk — the equivalent of smoking fifteen cig-
arettes a day,[28] and yet there has been a "precipitous"
decline in how many people make use of libraries,
community centers, and recreation centers.[29]

There are countless ways to connect. Each one starts
with reaching out.

4. **Purpose in life.** Purpose is unique to each person,
and difficult to define, but clearly, it involves self-
compassion in the form of giving yourself permission
to follow your deepest longings without letting these
longings become mere selfishness and self-absorption.

Still not sure what your purpose might be? Try reading *Purpose and Power in Retirement: New Opportunities
for Meaning and Significance* by Harold G. Koenig, M.D.
I especially like the twenty myths of aging that Koenig
refutes, including this one (p. 32) that connects "purpose" to Carter's call for "strong ties with other people."

Myth: It is natural to disengage from society and
withdraw from community involvement as one
grows older.

Fact: Older people who disengage from society or
withdraw from social interactions often do so because
they are depressed, angry, or otherwise emotionally
distressed and disappointed, having lost vision and
purpose for their lives. Disengagement is not part of
normal aging.

Discovering

The Care and Feeding of Curiosity

*Once we believe in ourselves, we can risk
curiosity, wonder, spontaneous delight, or
any experience that reveals the human spirit.*

— e. e. cummings

ON A SUNNY SEPTEMBER DAY, while walking with grandchildren aged two and four, I marveled that the autumn leaves drew them like magnets. Dozens of times, they ran back to me shouting, "Look! Look at this leaf! It's so red!" Another day, they collected chestnuts and, again, it was, "Look! Look how shiny this one is! And this one's a twin!" I returned home aware of how privileged I was to see the world anew through the eyes of a child. And the next time I went out, I too filled my pockets with chestnuts and brought home a bouquet of scarlet leaves.

The young are fascinated by almost everything that they see, hear, or touch. The sight of a bug crawling along the sidewalk, the feel of warm sand between fingers and toes, or even of water in the bath becomes a source of wonder. I love walking the parks and beaches with my grandchildren, sharing their excitement as they pick up a shell or a pebble or a twig, fascinated by its uniqueness in a world of diversity.

Curiosity marks the energetic elder every bit as much as it characterizes the very young. It is a trait we need not outgrow, no matter how hard society tries to push us to do so. In our school years, we learn that "being cool" trumps excitement, and that the prescribed curriculum should be met with boredom and disdain. Some of that may be a response to the nature of the material and its delivery, but I am certainly not the first teacher to have watched enthusiasm turn into yawns and sighs of resignation as childhood gives way to adolescence.

The narrowing down in school and in life is relentless. "Why?" quickly gives way to the factual "What?" and then to the computational "How much?" All too often, the inquisitive child morphs into a teen and then into a post-secondary student who must choose a future direction without having explored the options. Having selected English literature, the student may "progress" to the poetry of William Blake, which will have to be narrowed down much further in order to write a dissertation and to earn a "higher degree" of learning. Increasingly, schools and universities are seen as training camps for skilled labor instead of forums for questioning and discussion.

For many adults, the challenges of the workplace necessitate even further specialization. While it is true that adults need not and generally do not go into intellectual hibernation between ages eighteen and sixty-five, there are limits to everyone's time and energy. Curiosity about areas beyond our field of expertise often becomes a luxury.

In retirement, our curiosity can once again spring to life and flourish. As gifted artists have long intuited, wondering leads to creativity before it circles back to wonderment. A few years ago, while walking down a country lane in England, I vowed never to pass another rose without stopping to smell its sweetness. Now, I sometimes pause to marvel also at the intricacy of leaves, and beyond that, to contemplate, at least for a moment, the wonder of it all.

Just as it is for children, it is a major task for elders to move beyond the familiar. We must strengthen our own capacity for curiosity and for mental flexibility. Indeed, I see it as the essential counterbalance to the lessening of physical flexibility that is our usual fate. Perhaps it is when we can no longer say "I do, therefore I am" that we more fully embrace the Cartesian "I think, therefore I am." Alberto Manguel goes even further, claiming that curiosity is integral to, and inseparable from our humanity.

We imagine in order to exist, and we are curious in order to feed our imaginative desire. Imagination ... develops with practice, not through successes, which are conclusions and therefore blind alleys, but through failures, through attempts that prove to be mistaken and require new attempts that will also, if the stars are kind, lead to new failures. The histories of art and literature, like those of philosophy and science, are the histories of such enlightened failures. "Fail. Try again. Fail better" was Beckett's summation.[1]

To some degree, curiosity is innate. A spark of the small child remains alive in everyone. It is reflected countless times a day as we search for information on our electronic devices. Yet, like so much else, human curiosity needs to be nurtured in order to thrive. I love the First Nations legend of two wolves who dwell within the human heart. The wolf named *Insatiable Curiosity* competes ferociously with the one named *Mental Sloth*. Plaintively, the little boy asks: "But Grandpa, which is the stronger wolf? Which one will win?" The elder replies: "In truth, my child, it is the wolf that you feed."

One way to feed curiosity is to associate with people who are deeply involved in realms that lie beyond our own domain. Their interests will stimulate our own curiosity, for it is only human nature to wonder why someone cares so deeply about a topic or an activity.

Many seniors who took a science degree are now studying the humanities and filling in the gaps in their learning. Those with humanities degrees are back on campus too, taking science courses to better appreciate the workings of the natural world. Those with no interest in adding more letters to their name are signed up for "third age courses" of every description. They are attending "Philosopher's Cafés," public lectures, and every sort of discussion group that sparks their curiosity. Even those whose mobility is limited are opting to study from home via computer. They are busy blogging and connecting, indulging their curiosity through interactive sharing and online learning.

Curiosity is leading some seniors to travel extensively. The luxury cruise ship industry is booming, but so is travel in the company of genuine experts. One friend is currently in Greece with an archeologist, indulging her passion for the richness of the past. Another friend has just returned from the Arctic, aboard a ship replete with scientists who have specialized in northern affairs. A third friend and his wife have just returned from two years in Ghana, sharing their knowledge of agriculture with farmers desperate to make their land more productive. They traveled with the intention of giving but, hearing their enthusiasm for the people with whom they worked, it's clear that my friends gained far more than they gave.

Another excellent way to feed the wolf of curiosity is by indulging in pursuits that were impossible at an earlier stage of life. I have finally taken piano lessons, an unaffordable luxury in my childhood. Other retirees are joining marching bands or community orchestras, reviving musical training and skills that have long lain dormant. Some retirees are developing their artistic talents, expanding the medium through which they give expression to the self. I have just seen a stunning exhibit of woodcarvings by a former accountant, each consisting of a fusion of grains from among the countless varieties of trees that grow on planet earth.

Other seniors are learning to write, either to express their inner creativity or to set down memories of a past that will seem utterly foreign to future generations. I have just received these words, part of a letter to a grandson, written by my beloved cousin Herbert at age ninety-five:

> Curiosity will not kill an old cat, but at least this old cat purrs wistfully at the thought of marvels that he will never know and that may totally transform your life style, or that of your children. When I was your present

age, one of the outstanding adventure books was Jules Verne's *Around the World in Eighty Days*. Though published in the later decades of the nineteenth century and known as a classic, it still lit fires in the realm of phantasy in the 1920s; Lindbergh did not fly the Atlantic until 1927. Looking ahead, what wondrous secrets will be revealed to us by gravitational waves which we are beginning to discern, about 100 years after their prediction by Einstein? I envy you the opportunity to listen to their whisperings.

Recently, I met a Benedictine monk who spends his days visiting seniors in various care facilities. He expressed admiration for the "wonderment" that characterizes so many elders. Although many have physical limitations, he is awed by their curiosity and by their expressions of what he calls "conscious gratitude" for the richness of their world. They express gratitude for time free of distractions, time to devote to the contemplation of beauty, time to connect with others, time to wonder about the nature of the world of reality and the inner realms of spirit.

The later years are growing years but, this time it is not our parents and teachers who are in control. We determine our own development. We can live in awe of the universe and its wonders, or we can suffocate in our own stale sameness. The choice is always ours to make. Like the legendary wolf, the more curiosity is fed, the stronger it grows. The stronger it grows, the more alive we become.

―≈―

IDEA:

Childhood and elderhood invite us to feed our curiosity.

ACTION:

1. If you are fortunate to have grandchildren, learn with them even if they live at a distance. Let them teach you. Encourage them to tell you and show you what turns

them on. Show interest in them and in their world rather than expecting them to be interested in your life as it is and as it was.

2. Follow up on whatever catches your eye or hooks your mind. Was that bird a nuthatch or a bushtit, and would you know the difference? Is that orphanage in Mali or Malawi, and where will you help?

3. Shake up your thoughts and refresh your mind by moving beyond your area of expertise. Sign up for a class in something new, whether its astronomy, bridge, carpentry, or dance. For the housebound and the geographically challenged, the world of electronic learning is at your fingertips. Are you taking advantage of this miracle?

4. If you think there is some truth to the adage that "a new thing a day keeps the doctor away," try tracking your learning every day for the next week or two. Write down how you feel each time that you add an item to your store of knowledge, awareness, or understanding.

Creating Circles of Connectivity

We need others physically, emotionally, intellectually; we need them if we are to know anything, even ourselves.

— C. S. Lewis

THE CONFUCIAN PHILOSOPHER MENCIUS describes friends as "the siblings God never gave us."

I never had a sibling and, for many years, circumstances left me friendless. The result has been to make me intensely aware of the richness of my current life, one that includes a multiplicity of friendships.

How one defines friendship will vary from person to person, just as does all else. In my case, I have found that the level of intimacy expected of a friend has diminished with the years. I no longer experience the need to share every thought with a confidant as was the case in my teens, nor do I still feel the surge of hopefulness that accompanied my first reading of Montaigne's definition of friendship:

> But in the friendship I speak of, [our souls] mix and work themselves into one piece, with so universal a mixture, that there is no more sign of the seam by which they were first conjoined. If a man should importune me to give a reason why I loved him, I find it could not otherwise be expressed, than by making answer: because it was he, because it was I.²

Nowadays, I welcome into my life those whom Montaigne rather scornfully dismissed as mere acquaintances. At an age where loss often raises its ugly head, I find it wonderfully reassuring to know that new social connections also await. Much of retirement includes time to socialize.

Almost everywhere, I encounter people whose company I enjoy. There has hardly been a day that has not been enlivened by spending time with someone, either intentionally or by accident. Interesting people can be found in the most unexpected circumstances.

I think of the tough-looking man who extended a friendly smile in a coffee shop where there were no other tables available. Initially, seeing that every visible inch of his body was covered in tattoos, I was tempted to turn aside. Fortunately, my father's favorite saying came to mind: *Der Herrgott hat einen grossen Tiergarten.* This translates roughly as "Strange creatures inhabit this giant zoo that the Lord chose to create." My father used the expression to teach me to welcome difference and to treat everyone with kindness, regardless of how odd they might initially seem.

Boldly, I asked Mr. Heavily-Inked about his tattoos. He explained that he was trained in health care and had spent many years reaching out to isolated tribes in the Amazon. Next, he had worked in the mean streets of Caracas, one of the world's most violent cities. The tattoos had been a means of breaking down barriers and of generating trust. He had begun with a few highly visible images on his face and neck, and had gradually extended the artwork along his arms and legs until much of his body was covered. My casual encounter with this man turned into an extended lunch during which *National Geographic* sprang to life before my eyes.

One evening I met a couple exiting the same movie theater. We exchanged a few words about the film and opted to continue our conversation at an adjoining coffee shop, where we discovered many common interests. He is a diplomat who served Canada in many of the world's hotspots; she is a warmhearted woman, accomplished in her own right, yet she has been at his side in country after country. Now, we meet regularly, and I always look forward to hearing more about the experiences that have shaped them.

Everywhere, there are opportunities to meet new people, yet surveys indicate that social isolation is a major problem despite the fact that simply joining a club is as good for your health as quitting smoking, exercising, or losing weight. The Vancouver Foundation reports "a precipitous decline" in how many people made use of libraries, community or recreation centers in 2017, that only about one in four people took part in any kind of community or neighborhood project ... and that, in a city as diverse as ours, only about one in four people attended an ethnic or cultural event put on by an ethnic or cultural group different than their own. They conclude that "little happens when people stay home with their own kind, and aren't interested or engaged in what happens beyond their own front yard."[3]

I welcome time spent with people from other cultures and with people who simply trigger a warm surge in my heart. At the same time, my door is always open to old friends, and few activities can compare to our moments of simple togetherness.

After interviewing forty men and women between the ages of 75 and 100 considered role models for aging, Lyndsay Green concluded that social interaction lies at the core of healthy aging.

> Researchers aren't certain why, but they're finding a strong link between the health, well-being, and quality of life of older people, and the strength and quality of their social relationships.... There is also some startling research that loneliness can actually increase the risk of Alzheimer's. There is even speculation that those famously healthy Mediterranean people may be healthy, not because of their diet, but because they enjoy high levels of social interaction, and deep and sustaining emotional networks.[4]

Friends and people with whom we feel that spark of connection are a gift more precious than jewels. As the saying goes, "we all need to be somebody's somebody," and friends tell us that we matter in a world that often seems indifferent to our existence. Harold Kushner writes:

> Friendships are ... a way for us to be recognized as unique people, to be reassured that we are appreciated for who we are.... The fact that they are voluntary, easier to leave than family, marriage, or professional relationships, reassures us that people remain our friends because they genuinely like us.[5]

For me, it is a luxury to be with people whose company I enjoy, as opposed to simply tolerating sometimes prickly and difficult colleagues. In retirement, I get to choose my associates, as do they. We bond because we recognize the unique and positive qualities of the other. We listen, we laugh, we learn, and we loosen up while dwelling for a while in the company of those who enrich our being.

Connection involves more than just the presence of other bodies. One can sometimes sit in a group around a table, yet feel lonelier than ever. Besides, each of us has differing needs for companionship. A close friend gets all her energy from being with others, while I need plentiful time alone to digest the after-effects of social interaction. The trick is to find our own equilibrium, the right balance that enables us to spend quality time with others while leaving space to sit quietly with our own thoughts.

The wider our range of connectivity, the greater the likelihood that multiple facets of our own inner richness will surface. Sometimes, social banter that is purely light-hearted and superficial is what is needed. At other times, we long to express a personal viewpoint or to ask a serious question. I love the exchange of ideas that leads people to rethink their positions, and I often go home with a new bee in my bonnet. At other times, however, we all need a friend with whom to be alone, a confidant who will listen and understand. Only thus can we cope effectively with whatever life has thrown at us.

Sometimes, a spouse can serve as that confidant, but sometimes it is unwise to rely exclusively on one person. Doing so may put more of a burden on that relationship than it can bear. Harold Kushner cautions us not to place all our emotional needs on a single person. He points out that our sense of significance is enhanced when we know we are important beyond our immediate family.

> Our mates may be good at meeting many of our emotional needs, but not all. Our relationship with our children may suffer if we ask them to meet our emotional needs. That is why we need friends.[6]

Kushner's words resonated deeply with me. Both my parents felt compelled to "keep up appearances" in the presence of others, especially in the small group of fellow immigrants with whom they socialized. For my parents, it was only with me that they could vent their occasional frustrations with one another. I adored my father, and I had no outlet for the grief I experienced whenever my mother said things like "If it weren't for you, I'd leave him." Conversely, my father often unburdened himself on our regular Sunday morning walks, speaking of his sense of inadequacy and failure in a world of high-achieving men whose bravado he could not match. It was all too much for my tender years.

Reaching out beyond the immediate family often requires having a shared interest or activity. In retrospect, I feel such sadness for my immigrant parents whose exhausting work schedule, limited budget, and primitive English precluded developing such interests. Playing golf, tennis, or any sport would have been unthinkable to them. Attending concerts and developing the vocabulary of classical music was a luxury beyond their dreams. They worked all week, shopped for groceries and tended to house and garden on the weekend. They socialized only on Saturday night, always with the same small group of fellow immigrants. To these friends, they presented only one side of themselves, and they had little concept of the fact that each person is simultaneously multifaceted and hugely compartmentalized.

I often picture people as similar to old apothecary cabinets in which only one drawer at a time can be opened. We all contain a multitude of drawers, and no one person is capable of opening all our drawers. A little something always remains hidden, even from our loved ones. We, in turn, open one drawer of this person and another drawer of that person. There will always be drawers we cannot open, drawers whose contents remain a mystery.

Although I count the wide range of friends who are accessible to me as among the best features of aging, statistics indicate that many people, especially men, are lonelier than ever.

> Recently, the Movember Foundation carried out a survey ... investigating friendship and loneliness among men. The results are alarming, with only 11 percent of single men across the spectrum in their early 20s to late-middle age saying they had a friend to turn to in a time of crisis, the number rising to 15 percent for married men.[7]

Other research confirms that loneliness is spreading.

> In Vancouver, residents recently listed social isolation as their most pressing concern. ... In the United States, two studies showed that 40 percent of people say they're lonely, a figure that has doubled in 30 years. ... The issue isn't just social, it's a public-health crisis in waiting. If you suffer from chronic loneliness, you run the risk of illness and premature death.[8]

Study after study indicates that many men do not have even a single friend in whom they can confide, and that young men in particular find heterosexual social life so problematic they have retreated from relationships altogether, despite fears of ending up alone. One young man is quoted as considering himself lucky to have been born in a slightly earlier era. At the ripe age of thirty-two, he states that "pornography has become ubiquitous in the life of young men, and it is stunting them ... At least I was old enough to have had real relationships and to know that porn is not really real."9

Whether one is young or old, making new friends is not always easy. That reality was driven home to me by the film *That Evening Sun*, which begins with Hal Holbrook in the role of an octogenarian in a nursing home. Sadly he sits, observing people he views as his "fellow inmates," who keep busy with cards or puzzles or knitting while others doze or stare blindly into space. In the next scene, he is carrying his small suitcase and trudging along the country road that leads to his erstwhile home. For ninety minutes, I was privileged to borrow his eyes. I saw the rutted driveway and the old homestead as lovingly as did he. Memories filled the dusty corners of his barn, and imagined smells warmed the kitchen where his wife used to bake apple pie. The imagined aroma, along with much else from the past, was a reminder of the void left in his heart and in his life by the loss of his wife. But returning to her kitchen would not bring her back. He needed to fill the void by other means. He needed to move forward rather than seek refuge in the past.

Like the hero of the film, most of us rate love and connection ahead of wealth as the source of true happiness. What we fear is going after it directly, thereby exposing our vulnerability to others. Here's how psychologists John Cacioppo and William Patrick explain it:

> It is hard for most of us to be articulate about our emotions under the best of circumstances. It is that much harder when we have intense sensations of threat flooding our body with stress hormones. Accordingly, a great many of us spend a great portion of our lives acting a bit like agitated wind-up dolls, walking into the same walls again and again, wondering why we are trapped inside such a small, lonely room — a room that we ourselves have inadvertently helped design.10

Thus, many of us are inadvertently the authors and designers of our own loneliness. The first time I had coffee with a small cluster of my gym-mates, they were discussing a film they had viewed at someone's home the previous Saturday night. A week later, only the title of the film had changed. After the third week of cinematic review, I felt so unwelcome that I considered quitting the gym. Instead, I decided to express my pain at not being included. To my great surprise, the host of these gatherings was devastated. It had never been his intention to exclude me; he simply hadn't thought of asking me to join them. The host is now a friend, and my life is the richer for it.

This experience bears out the truism that the protective crouch may be a human default position, but it rarely serves us well. Had I not cast aside my defensive shield, I would have missed out on countless gatherings of an ever-expanding group that now takes pains to ensure everyone feels welcome and included.

—*∿∿*—

IDEA:

> Sometimes, inadvertently, we become the authors and designers of our own loneliness.

ACTION:

1. Go places alone, at least sometimes. If you are always with a companion, you are less likely to talk to the person sitting beside you at the concert.

2. At any large gathering, approach new people. You will seldom leave a large gathering without having met someone you'd like to talk to again.

3. Don't say goodbye to someone who sparks your interest without asking for a business card, email, or phone number. Within twenty-four hours, follow up with a message saying how much you enjoyed your chat, and suggesting you meet for coffee. You'll rarely receive a refusal.

4. Each time you leave the house, reach out to one other person, young or old. Compliment the woman in the wheelchair on her jaunty red hat. Ask the youngster on the bus whether he has lots of homework in that bulky backpack. Why assume a defensive crouch, or expect others to break the ice?

Cultivating Compassion

*Compassion is the chief law of
human existence.*

— Fyodor Dostoyevsky

WHEN I FIRST STUMBLED upon the above Dostoyevsky quote,
I found it puzzling. *Compassion as the chief law of human existence?* How could that possibly apply to the competitive, dog-eat-dog
world that seems to be our reality? Is compassion innate, or must it be
learned? How is compassion different from empathy, and why does it
seem so clearly present among the elders in my social circles?

As always, with my love of language, I began to research the word
itself. The Latin root of compassion is *cum patior*, to suffer with. In
German, the equivalent word is *Mitleid*, which clearly means "to suffer with (the other)." German also has the word *Mitgefühl*, literally
"feeling with" (the other). *Merriam-Webster* states that "compassion is
broader than empathy because it refers to both an understanding of
another's pain and the desire to somehow mitigate that pain."

Theologian Matthew Fox takes that definition a step further:

> Compassion is not pity in the sense that our culture
> understands pity. It is not a feeling sorry for someone,
> nor is it a preoccupation with pain. ... Pity is about emot-
> ing and feeling without including actual relieving of the
> causes of another's pain.[11]

The emphasis on action helped me to understand both why compassion matters so greatly, and why I see it reflected so clearly in the

older adults whose company I enjoy. They have evolved both personally and communally. Many have let go of traits that once plagued
them: anger, impatience, impulsivity, self-centeredness, self-pity, and
the like. They have gradually, if imperfectly, replaced these with
increased thoughtfulness, a sense of humor, tolerance, greater gener-
osity, and a willingness to accept the foibles of others. They are thus
more likely to embody compassion and to act accordingly.

My own experience tells me that aging brings a hormonal and
glandular balance lacking during those years of impetuosity that
Goethe so aptly labeled *Sturm und Drang*. Gradually, romantic excess
gives way to a softer, more even-tempered nature and to a perspective
that is less impetuous and more thoughtful. Instead of resenting individuals and institutions, I look back now and see them as the stimulus
for inner strength and for personal change that has ultimately been
beneficial.

While some people do get cranky, cynical, and self-centered with
age, my experience is that such folks are not the norm. Often, they
have known nothing but frustration. The dissolution of their dreams
has made them bitter, and so, like mistreated dogs, they snarl. At
every age, some people barricade themselves behind high walls,
let no one approach, and become totally self-absorbed. Here's how
Daniel Goleman, who coined the concept of emotional intelligence,
describes the phenomenon:

> Self-absorption in all its forms kills empathy, let alone
> compassion. When we focus on ourselves, our world con-
> tracts as our problems and preoccupations loom large.
> But when we focus on others, our world expands. Our
> own problems drift to the periphery of the mind and so
> seem smaller, and we increase our capacity for connec-
> tion — or compassionate action.[12]

Elders who have led reasonably satisfying lives are anything but
self-absorbed. Frequently, I find myself performing acts of kindness

that, once, I would have been too self-absorbed to consider. Moreover, I catch myself regularly looking beyond myself to friends and acquaintances who deliberately pursue a life of compassionate involvement. Like the common cold, I find myself "catching the bug." These people inspire me to do more and to be more than I used to be. As a result, my world keeps expanding.

Scientific observers are challenging the assumption that evolution has conditioned us to be selfish, greedy, and competitive. Instead, they are finding increasing evidence that humans are hardwired for compassion. Scientists and thinkers whose findings have made their way into a scholarly book entitled *The Compassionate Instinct: The Science of Human Goodness* make a convincing argument that "taken together, our strands of evidence suggest that compassion is deeply rooted in human nature and has a biological basis in brain and body."[13] What's more, compassion can be cultivated.

Jonathan Haidt, moral psychologist and professor of ethical leadership at NYU-Stern, has reached a similar conclusion about human nature:

> We've been told for fifty years now that human beings are fundamentally selfish. ... Some people actually believe that a woman should shout "fire" if she's being raped, on the grounds that [no one will] come out to investigate unless they fear for their own lives. It's not true. We may spend most of our waking hours advancing our own interests, but we all have the capacity to transcend self-interest.[14]

At our coffee gathering this morning, we elders discussed how to transcend self-interest and create a kinder world. Some of the discussion centered on ways to use technology more effectively in the service of humanity. Primarily, however, we strove to come up with concrete answers to the core question: If change can only start with the individual, how can each of us become more compassionate?

When I got home, I decided to email the question to friends whose compassion is exemplary for me. Here are some of their responses:

a. If you ask me, the problem is that many people empathize with others, but few do something about it. Compassion means more of us need to stop talking and start walking.

b. Having the intention is most important. Keeping it in mind is next. Having compassion for yourself when you do not act perfectly is third.

c. Listen more, talk less, but speak out when you hear someone being intolerant of another person or group. In that case, silence becomes complicity, and you are sitting passively while Rome burns.

d. When you are down, volunteer to help others. When you feel great, ditto. I don't think much about pain, just about loving people and trying to make them feel better. In turn, that makes me feel worthwhile.

e. Compassion starts with empathy, and empathy starts with understanding — I am making a conscious effort to broaden my understanding rather than jump on the bandwagon of blame and condemnation. I am making a conscious effort to be less judgmental and to understand other people's perspectives.

f. I believe that it is our recognition of the goodness in others that propels us forward. I also believe that each of us can become more compassionate simply by associating with people whose good qualities inspire us and bring out the best in us.

g. We cannot change others, but we can strive to change ourselves in positive ways. Compassion is the starting point.

h. I seek concrete ways to support individuals and organizations that promote healing in the world. If someone comes to my door to raise funds for a cause, I send no one away completely empty-handed. I have increased my monthly donations to a number of other organizations whose work strikes me as particularly important. It may ultimately be selfish, because I know that these small and steady acts of compassion will not change the world. Still, they help me feel better about myself, and less guilty about having access to all that is mine to enjoy.

My fellow octogenarian Harold Kushner brings compassion into focus by pointing out that setting off a bomb in a crowd of civilians is not merely against the law; it violates our sense of what it is to be a human being.

> Over the centuries, our understanding of those to whom we owe sympathy has expanded from family to community to nation, and finally to all humanity. The definition of acceptable or unacceptable behavior may vary slightly from one society to another, but a basic awareness of good and bad behavior seems universal.[15]

Innate compassion dictates that we suffer when others suffer. Research is providing increasing evidence that Kushner's "basic awareness of good and bad behavior" is present at birth.

> Morality is not just something that people learn. It is something we are all born with. At birth, babies are endowed with compassion, with empathy, with the beginnings of a sense of fairness. The earliest signs are the glimmerings of empathy and compassion — pain at the pain of others, which you can see pretty soon after birth. Once they're capable of coordinated movement, babies will often try to soothe others who are suffering, by patting and stroking.[16]

There is precious little that an infant can do, but as elders, we have time and skills with which to soothe others who are suffering. Sometimes, we can even take an additional step to ensure a decline in suffering. As Martin Luther King Jr. once reminded us, "True compassion is more than flinging a coin to a beggar; it comes to see that an edifice which produces beggars needs restructuring." Seeing that need, wanting as elders to restructure the existing edifice, that is the flowering of our innate human goodness. It calls to us from deep within, awakening the urge to reach out to those who suffer. We long to alleviate pain and wherever possible, to eliminate its causes. As William Blake said so poignantly in 1789:

> Can I see another's woe,
> And not be in sorrow too?
> Can I see another's grief,
> And not seek for kind relief?

Volunteering is not a four-letter word. Cultivating compassion, finding ways to apply our skills, acting on our longing to be decent, caring humans, using our time to lessen the pain of others, these are among the greatest privileges of aging.

—⁓—

IDEA:

> Compassion may well be the only attribute that each of us has and each of us can give freely, no strings attached. It requires no money, no solution, not even that you love your neighbor as yourself. Given freely, compassion makes a huge difference to both the recipients and to how you feel about yourself.

ACTION:

1. Seek ways to express your compassion not in grandiose gestures or heroic deeds, but through acts of micro-kindness. For details, see Erin Anderssen, "The Compassion Deficit," *Globe and Mail*, Dec. 24, 2017.

2. Look for compassion in those you choose as your companions, and look upon aging as an opportunity to associate with people who inspire you.

3. List the ways that you are already demonstrating micro-kindness. Remind yourself that aging invites us to bring our compassion to the table. Together, we can work to build that morally remarkable culture of which we dreamt in our youth.

4. Focus on opportunities to convert compassion into action. Here are just a few of the countless ways to make a difference:

1. Volunteerism
- Volunteer Canada: www.volunteer.ca/
- Volunteers of America: www.voa.org/

2. Indigenous Reconciliation
- Truth and Reconciliation Commission of Canada: www.trc.ca/websites/trcinstitution/index.php?p=3
- The Advocates for Human Rights www.theadvocatesforhumanrights.org/volunteer

3. The Environment
- Environmental Volunteer Opportunities in Canada: www.planetfriendly.net/volunteers/vol.php
- Volunteer Environmental Conservation Projects Abroad: www.projects-abroad.org/volunteer-projects/conservation-and-environment/

4. Refugees

- Canadian Council for Refugees:
  www.ccrweb.ca/en/get-involved
- International Rescue Committee:
  www.rescue.org/volunteer

5. Seniors

- International Volunteer Opportunities for Seniors with Projects Abroad:
  www.projects-abroad.ca/how-it-works/older-volunteers/
- Senior Volunteering Abroad When You're Young at Heart (for women):
- www.women-on-the-road.com/senior-volunteering.html

Choosing Happiness

*Very little is needed to make a happy life; it is
all within yourself, in your way of thinking.*

— Marcus Aurelius

BEING HAPPY WHEN YOU ARE HAPPY IS EASY. The challenge is to
retain the conviction that life is worth living even when things
don't go according to plan. I am often tempted to slide beyond sadness into a deep funk that is hardly helpful. This is especially true as
I watch contemporaries cope with disease and physical limitations,
or when I listen to younger friends wrestle with personal and professional problems that threaten to flatten them. Humorist Anne Hines
labels such battles "tsunamis of the soul," and asks how it is possible
that reasonable, self-assured people can be leveled by these sudden
bouts of low self-esteem.

> The answer is, of course, that no reasonable person has
> much self-esteem at all. History is littered with tales of
> those who achieved fame and glory... yet who succumbed
> to feeling poorly about themselves. Marilyn Monroe
> doubted her looks. Beethoven questioned his musical
> ability. Mother Teresa ... suffered frequent bouts of depres-
> sion and misgivings. If these luminaries couldn't escape
> the tsunamis of the soul, is there hope for the rest of us?[17]

When we are bowled over by adversity, we are both humbled and
reminded of the frailty of our inner being. Such setbacks, however,
are also a clarion call to get back on our feet and to move forward, be

it ever so slowly. In life, there is no real way to stand still. Time does not stop for us, no matter how precious or how punishing a given moment may be.

I hasten here to distinguish between temporary moroseness and genuine late-onset depression, a serious illness for many seniors that requires meaningful medical intervention. Dr. Deborah Serani writes that "depression is not synonymous with adjectives like blue, sad, dejected, down, melancholy, or unhappy" nor is it "an experience that fades with the next sunrise or can be shaken off with a newfound attitude." Rather, she continues, "depression ... decays your mind, siphons your soul, and crushes the glimpse of possibility, hope, and freedom at every turn."[18]

I hasten also to clarify what I mean by happiness, a concept that means vastly different things to different people. For some, it is an innate cheerfulness, an ability to laugh at life's perverse jokes, and to steer along a path that includes lots of fun. I barely know the meaning of fun, and although I love to lose myself in absorbing activities like chess, duplicate bridge, or downhill skiing, I don't seem to have fun the way others do. Unlike many female friends, I've never learned to giggle or titter, and although I smile a lot, I rarely laugh.

To a considerable extent, that soberness is cultural. My immigrant parents were serious people. *Das Leben ist ernst* was a household dictum. *Life is no laughing matter*, they'd often say with a sigh. They wondered why Canadians laughed so much. "What's so funny?" my parents would ask. I was astounded recently to learn from friends born in the UK that in some homes, humor is actually taught and encouraged as a social skill.

If I rarely laugh, if I don't play mindless games, and if I barely know the meaning of fun, can I still call myself happy? I can and I do. In what was for me a life-changing book, Martin Seligman describes the nature of "authentic happiness."[19] He points out that each of us has a set point of happiness that is inborn. Despite life's inevitable peaks and valleys, we revert to that set point. That is why rich people are often no happier than the disadvantaged, and why the euphoria of winning the lottery fades so quickly.

I'm unlikely to win the lottery, but that's because I don't buy tickets. While I'm deeply aware of the degree to which Good Fortune smiles upon me in my personal life, I recognize that externals are only part of the answer to my happiness. My happiness flows from a force deep within, from an ability to hold fast to those moments that leaven and lighten me in heart, mind, and spirit.

Still, world events frequently cause my thoughts to go into a tailspin. In vain I remind myself that I am inclined to imagine shadows as monsters waiting to pounce. Equally in vain, a friend often suggests that before I panic, I should first ask "Helen, has it happened yet?" She reminds me that panic leads both to irrational action and to its opposite, a state of total paralysis. It is only by facing our fears that we have any hope of overcoming them.

I remembered this on a recent evening when a grandchild stumbled out of her bedroom, sobbing about monsters hiding in her closet. I opened wide the door and assured her that I have skills to defeat monsters and demons. A favourite technique is to demolish them before they have a chance to grow, as they do when we try to ignore them. If we open the door, if we shine a bit of light upon them, they tend to disappear back into the woodwork.

My own monsters tend to be powerful people who have either been chosen by or inflicted upon simple civilians who are just trying to survive. Since shooting these monsters is not among my options, I work at neutralizing their impact through action. Sometimes this means fund-raising, sometimes it means political activism or peaceful protest, and sometimes it means hands-on help. Whatever the monstrosity, ignoring it is not the solution.

The early Greeks had already discerned that at every age in life, we can choose how to deal with demons and darkness. In his sweeping overview of human philosophy, psychology, and neuroscience, Richard Precht takes us back to Epicurus, who died in 270 BCE.

Epicurus had already highlighted human strategies to maximize energy and to focus on what really matters:

> One such strategy is ... to savor the many small moments in life just as fully as the big ones. ... It is not always possible to experience great pleasure, but one can try to reduce the feelings of displeasure by keeping needless worrying about the future to a minimum, reining in one's ambitions, and restricting one's longings for money and possessions, all of which yield little joy.[20]

Aging has made me a connoisseur of life. It has taught me to savor not what is rare or high-priced, but what is ordinary. The small moments that sometimes overwhelm me with heart-stopping joy. An incredible blue-sky day. The first sip of my morning coffee. The laughter of family and friends. Whenever I am walking in the woods with a boisterous dog, whenever I sit on a log at the beach while the sun dips slowly below the horizon and paints the sky with hues no artist could capture, whenever I stroll through a harvest market where farm-fresh produce overwhelms with its ripe richness, whenever my grandchildren burst through the doorway to give me a hug, or whenever I am engaged in any number of absorbing activities, I so often have an overwhelming sense of not wanting to be anywhere in the world except exactly where I am at this moment.

Still, I know that happiness is an elusive creature, one that I glimpse from time to time, yet one that vanishes whenever I try to seize it. As Precht points out, such thoughts as mine are hardly original. They have plagued humans for centuries. Precht links Epicurus to advances in positive psychology, a field of study that seeks to train people to become happier. Current brain research confirms that happiness must be produced actively. It does not simply arise on its own, nor is the absence of stress, pain, or problems enough to make us happy. Precht continues:

> Ecstatic harmony doesn't last ... A desperate attempt to prolong [it] can cumulate in destructive cravings for

drugs, sex, or success ... Expansive feelings of happiness are "isles of the blessed" in the ocean of our lives, but we cannot use them as on-going means to a successful life.[21]

In our society, the successful life is always relative, and it stems primarily from comparing ourselves to others. Somehow, as elders, most of us have stumbled into material self-sufficiency, whether our parents were simple working folk or among the moderately prosperous. We worked hard, we became responsible, and we scrambled our way up the ladder. We knew that there is no bed of roses. Every venture has its upside and its downside. "To venture causes anxiety, but not to venture is to lose one's self," said Kierkegaard. There is no way around that particular dilemma.

Mark Nepo writes: "The truth is that, given enough time, life bestows its gifts, a drop at a time, if we can find the courage to stay open to the mysterious flow that is larger than any one event."[22]

We have all received these gifts, even when we have failed to remain open. Conversely, we have also known many moments of what I call "the four D's": Disappointment, Disillusionment, Despair, and Death itself. No one is immune, nor is anyone exempt. Still, it is only by connecting with both life's gifts and its challenges that we earn and experience our moments of happiness. Like walking a tightrope, living with loss while staying open to the "mysterious flow that is larger than any one event" is not easy. Nonetheless, our future well-being depends on maintaining that fragile balance.

Here's how Sean Meshorer, a leading figure in the personal development movement, expresses the situation:

> Neither our minor issues nor major traumas need define us, let alone destroy us. We can use them as catalysts to making ourselves better, happier, and stronger people. ... The more we dwell on any positives, even the smallest and slightest, the easier it is to integrate that negative memory into our present experience.[23]

Whether our past has been painful or joyful, we must come to terms with it so that we can live in our present, which is all that we can be assured of having. In the process of acceptance, I hope that I will let go of whatever anger against myself still lingers. I still need to exercise self-compassion, and to stop blaming myself for all the times that I have failed. I need to remember that the words, penned in the 1600s by Thomas Browne, are still applicable:

> How shall we expect charity toward others, when we are uncharitable to ourselves? Charity begins at home, is the voice of the world, yet is everyman his greatest enemy, and as it were, his executioner.

Charity towards myself begins with banishing pointless regret. Instead of wishing that I had seen more clearly in the past, I need to concentrate on seeing more clearly now. I must accept that at every age and stage, I have done my best, and that tomorrow, I will continue to do my best.

If I wish to experience Seligman's "authentic happiness," then I must also keep in mind the important distinction between rapidly diminishing pleasures (the first bite of chocolate, the sigh of relief as I enter my front door) and what Seligman calls the "gratifications." These are activities like "three sets of tennis, or participating in a clever conversation, or reading Richard Russo,"[24] which not only require skill and effort, but also offer the possibility of failing.

Too often, we opt for distraction even though we know that action is the route to real happiness. Colin Beavan's experience lends support to the view that happiness is a by-product of action:

> When we stop limiting ourselves and hiding our light under old stories, we have a better chance of helping ourselves and the world. When we choose to live according to our values, people pay attention and the ripples spread. When we take responsibility for the world's problems — accept our ability to respond — others are

inspired to do so. We feel as though we matter. We get happier lives.[25]

Because we are doers by nature, we long to do something, if possible with or for those we love. That is why action by our own choice gives meaning to who we are and trumps all else in making us happy. Despite the effort involved, happiness is using our natural capacities to the fullest extent possible. Peter Block calls this "growing up" as citizens of the free world.

> When we finally grow up — at whatever age, and so often not until retirement, our first order of business is to decide that our deepest purpose will only find expression when we transform the culture and the institutions we have inherited. This is what it means to be a citizen and to grow up.... We choose activism. We dive into the world and swim beneath the surface. We are peers joining together to change the world, not individuals negotiating with our leaders.[26]

I see happiness as both a choice and a consequence. It flows from the decisions we make, from what we learn by experience, and from the challenges we set ourselves. It requires us to engage all our faculties while remaining open to the possibility of failure.

From time to time, in my striving, I will stumble in the dark. Still, I hope my hand and my thoughts will always reach for the light.

—◌◌◌—

IDEA:

> Happiness is an elusive creature that tends to vanish the moment we shine the light of consciousness upon it. If, as brain research increasingly confirms, the mere absence of stress, pain, or problems is not enough to make us happy, that places the responsibility in our own hands.

ACTION:

1. Don't confuse surface joviality with what may be happiness for you. Some people seem to find joy easily and
   naturally, but for others, happiness is a choice. It flows
   from the decisions they make, from the challenges
   they set themselves, and from the attitude they take in
   the face of reality. Such happiness does not preclude
   feeling deep sadness at times, nor does it necessitate
   wearing a mask of surface cheer.

2. Practice gratitude on a daily basis at a regular time
   and place. Perhaps when you turn out the light, think
   of three good things that happened that day. These
   might be actions, experiences, or simply moments of
   awareness. Sunlight sparkling on a snowy landscape.
   The happy shouts and laughter of children on a play-
   ground. The glimpse of a flower, a bird, or a butterfly.
   Music. Sinking into a warm tub. Someone's thoughtfulness, including your own.

3. Do something, especially for those you love, whether
   that circle is narrow or wide enough to encompass the
   globe. We are doers by nature, which is why action
   springing from free will and our own choice trumps all
   else in bringing us happiness.

4. Remind yourself that good things will happen and bad
   things will happen, but the level of overall happiness is
   yours to choose.

Daring

Reaching Out

To travel is to take a journey into yourself.

— Danny Kaye

AS A STRONG BELIEVER IN CROSS-CULTURAL OUTREACH, I was delighted when my daughter accepted an invitation to lecture at a university in China. I was even more delighted when she invited me as chaperone during her working hours for Ben and Zach, her ten-year-old twins. Although I was almost an octogenarian, I leapt for joy.

The trip did not disappoint. Indeed, it exceeded all expectations. Mark Twain's words still ring true.

> Travel is fatal to prejudice, bigotry, and narrow-mindedness, and many of our people need it sorely on these accounts. Broad, wholesome, charitable views of men and things cannot be acquired by vegetating in one little corner of the earth all one's lifetime.

While I greatly treasure every hard-won nanometer of our democracy, China nonetheless held up a mirror that compelled me to re-examine a number of assumptions. A few examples:

1. For years, I had accepted the maxim that communism is totally without merit and that democracy is the sister of perfection. Today, while I have no desire to live under a totalitarian regime, I experience serious discomfort with some aspects of our democracy. I am no longer so certain that "our way" is as flawless as I had been led to believe. Moreover, I

attach new meaning to the biblical caution that only those who are free of sin are entitled to cast the first stone.

2. Having become accustomed to reading about human rights abuse in China, I was shocked to pick up an English-language newspaper with banner headlines asking "How Dare They?" The subsequent article cataloged shameful instances of racism and human rights abuse in the US and in other "free-world" countries.

3. Having read endless accounts of China as a major polluter unconcerned about global warming, I was amazed to see solar panels on city buildings and wind turbines dotting the countryside with a frequency similar to what I had seen in Germany and Denmark.

4. The rapid transit system that we used wherever we went made me ashamed of our urban rush hour, where single-occupant cars inch their way along clogged streets and high-ways to reach single family homes. In Shanghai, the subway system may well be among the most advanced in the world. Sixteen lines of smoke-free, air-conditioned trains glide on tracks shielded by glass panels, which prevent passengers (and my rambunctious young charges) from falling onto the tracks. Meanwhile, back in Canada, either because they were car owners or because they had some ax to grind with the decision-makers, BC voters were rejecting a proposed regional levy to fund rapid transit. It made me think how selfishly we often vote, and how we no longer even question the fact that political parties cater to that selfishness by promising favors to targeted groups at the expense of what is right for the city, the province, or the country as a whole.

5. China held up a mirror that led me to re-examine the history I had been taught in high school and university. Day by day, it became more difficult to view the West as having brought

enlightenment to backward Asians. Awed, I stood at a site marking the start of the Silk Road, reading a sign describing the thriving marketplace that had arisen here BCE as a "site for trading material goods as well as a conduit for the spread of knowledge, ideas, and culture." As if to clarify the point, another sign insisted that "here, in this marketplace, the spiritual wealth and the cultural treasures of humanity were traded."

6. From museum exhibits, I learned that by the mid-nineteenth century, the British East India Company was heavily in debt. This was partly due to the cost of conquering and occupying India, and partly due to the UK's insatiable demand for tea and other goods from China. Even though China's emperor had issued an edict stating clearly that "opium is a poison, undermining our good customs and morality, and its use is prohibited by law," the British insisted, ultimately by force of arms, that opium (conveniently grown in India) be allowed into the country. Soon, China was saddled with a serious addiction problem and the trade deficit morphed into a huge surplus for Britain. This ugly bit of history springs to mind now when I spot references to the opioid crisis that is killing Canadians in epidemic numbers.[1]

7. China is not simply a materialistic culture, nor is it merely "the nation of imitators" that I had been led to expect. From a sign on the wall of an art museum whose twelve floors were abuzz with thousands of excited students, I copied this statement:

> Art education is a lifelong career. For most people, art is crucial, because art teaches not only ideas and knowledge, but builds character and enhances morality. A legitimate education must be able to produce people who both think and create.

Wow! People who both think and create! I could not help contrasting this with the shortsightedness evident in Canada's education system, where school districts routinely attempt to cut costs by axing art and music programs, considered to be mere "frills." Have I ever in Canada seen it clearly written that a *legitimate education must be able to produce people who both think and create*?

8. Finally, having read repeated media reports describing Chinese people as greedy, self-seeking individualists, I must publicly proclaim that my experience was the complete opposite. Even though I am well-aware of the dangers of generalizing from a handful of individuals to a group level, even though I know full well that no nation, religion, tribe or other group exclusively contains only good people or only rotten apples, still, I found myself overwhelmed by a degree of honesty and a level of kindness that outstripped anything I have experienced elsewhere.

   Several times, shopkeepers chased me down the street because I had forgotten my water bottle, or I had left a bit of change on the counter. In personal encounters where I had the opportunity to share a meal or to have some form of meaningful contact, I could feel people reach out to me across the language barrier and embrace me with an emotional largesse that spoke from the heart.

I had occasion several times to think about selflessness not just on a personal level, but on a broader scale. In one of the museums, I spotted a painting of impoverished residents of Shanghai sharing their meager food rations with the Jews fleeing Nazi Germany. Despite limited resources, the city accepted twenty-five thousand Jewish refugees between 1937 and 1941, the period when all the great powers closed their doors and Canada's policy toward the Jews became "None Is Too Many."[2]

The painting led me to seek out the small Jewish Museum where a plaque in English and in Chinese script bore these words by Nobel Peace Prize Winner Elie Wiesel: *The past is in the present, but the future is still in our hands.*

I looked at my grandsons and at the two incredibly kind, incredibly sensitive students who stood at my side, and whispered a small "Amen." May they and others like them find the courage to guide our future world wisely and well.

⸺⁓⸺

Upon returning to Canada, I was disoriented. From my livingroom window, I gazed at empty sidewalks on both sides of a street lined with parked cars, even though each home in my area has a double- or even a triple-car garage.

An irksome noise broke my reverie. It was early July, and only a few leaves had fallen to spoil the perfection of a neighbor's small patch of lawn, but armed with a leaf blower, he chased each leaf to the street where it lay in the gutter awaiting the next gust of wind that would return it to his or to another's lawn. Large ear-protectors shielded him from the racket.

My mind flipped back to China where people used rakes to keep the parks clean, green, and peacefully inviting. I watched many Chinese workers wielding only a twig broom with which they kept the streets spotless. There seemed to be a task for everyone, and even those whose skills were limited had opportunities to be useful.

Repeatedly, my thoughts also returned to the extraordinary helpfulness we encountered daily. In Beijing, where we were completely on our own, without a word of Mandarin and without helpful student volunteers from the university, we were nonetheless treated to incessant acts of kindness.

No sooner had our high-speed train (the twins had explained to me that it travels on magnetism with wheels that need not touch the ground) reached the station, than we spotted a large sign bearing my daughter's name. The closest attendant asked us to wait, and moments later, we were greeted by a young woman who identified herself as Jing, the former classmate of one of my daughter's current graduate students. Jing had come to welcome us to Beijing and planned to accompany us to our hotel to ensure we were comfortably settled. But first, she had two lovely red gift boxes for the twins.

I'm not sure I can picture the reverse happening in Canada. Would one of my former university classmates in Toronto go to the airport to welcome a complete stranger from another land? A stranger with nothing to offer my former classmate in the way of career advancement, and no evident commonalities or interests? Would that former Canadian classmate arrive bearing gifts?

As we made our way by subway and then on foot, we learned that Jing was well-established on her own career path, that she had little prospect of visiting Canada, and that she had absolutely no vested interest in cultivating our goodwill. Nonetheless, she gave freely. She not only insisted upon taking us to a memorable dinner but also on paying the entire tab. We expressed our thanks and said our goodbyes, not expecting to see her again. However, on our very last day in Beijing, Jing returned to our hotel, once more bearing gifts in red boxes. We begged her to stay, but her time was limited. She was on her lunch hour and had to rush back.

Back in Vancouver, I thought of Jing and of the many Chinese people I met and grew to value as people. I reflected on the fact that I rarely have such encounters in my neighborhood. Despite Vancouver's claim to being "the most Asian city outside Asia," there exists an "us/them" mentality, an invisible barrier that limits our interactions. Is the fault ours for being less than welcoming, or is it a case of newcomers clustering with those who speak their language? Are Canadians perhaps not as friendly as we like to think?

I draw upon fond memories now. Memories of parks in China where women pulled me into their morning exercise routines and where men asked me to dance to music emanating from a radio, where people greeted me and returned my smiles wherever I went. In many ways, my home town now feels like a lonely place.

Like aging itself, travel provides an opportunity for growth. It is much more than merely seeing the sights and collecting photos or souvenirs. Travel changes us by challenging our preconceptions. It enables us to learn about other people and other places, but it also provides a mirror in which to view ourselves and our own country. It invites us to look at how we engage — or fail to engage — with strangers whose language and culture differ from our own. Both travel and aging can be an impetus to see through a different lens. Both can prompt us to act in accordance with new insights and awareness. As elders, that inward journey is among the precious gems that we treasure ever more greatly.

— ∿ —

IDEA:

> Travel holds up a mirror that reflects our prejudices and preconceptions. It invites us to go inward, as a nation, as a culture, and as individuals in order to discover what we might learn from one another.

A FEW FAVOURITE QUOTES ON TRAVEL:

- *To travel is to discover that everyone is wrong about other countries.*

  — Aldous Huxley

- *Whenever you find yourself on the side of the majority, it's time to pause and reflect.*

  — Mark Twain

- *Perhaps travel cannot prevent bigotry, but by demonstrating that all peoples cry, laugh, eat, worry, and die, it can introduce the idea that if we try and understand each other, we may even become friends.*

  — Maya Angelou

- *All travel has its advantages. If the passenger visits better countries, he may learn to improve his own.*

  — Samuel Johnson

- *To travel is to take a journey into yourself.*

  — Danny Kaye

- *Life is either a daring adventure or nothing.*

  — Helen Keller

- *Travel is more than the seeing of sights; it is a change that goes on, deep and permanent, in the ideas of living.*

  — Miriam Beard

- *Don't listen to what they say. Instead, go see.*

  — Chinese Proverb

Embracing Travel

*Twenty years from now you will be more
disappointed by the things you didn't do. So
throw off the bowlines. Sail away from the
safe harbor. Catch the trade wind in your
sails. Explore. Dream. Discover.*

— Mark Twain

TRAVEL LURES US, especially after we retire. Many people put it
at the top of their bucket list. It is part of the urge to expand our
horizons and to understand the world at a deeper level. I have always
viewed other people as my teachers, and the more sharply they dif-
fered from me, the greater the likelihood that they presented a chance
for me to learn new attitudes and approaches.

For me, travel represents the opportunity to meet people whose
experience has been different from my own. Galleries, museums,
monuments interest me only to the degree that they reflect another
way of perceiving and relating to the world. Travel lures me to explore
difference.

I was on the street not far from home when I saw an acquaintance and stopped to chat. She was on her way to get vaccines for
an upcoming trip to India where her geologist husband routinely
spends winters when frozen Canadian terrain precludes mineral
exploration. When I expressed interest, she suggested that I join
them for part of the winter. I could have hesitated, but this seemed
like the perfect moment to adhere to my motto of "When in doubt,
say 'yes' to opportunity."

And thus, I found myself in India, traveling not with fellow tourists by air-conditioned coach, but by local transport. For short distances, this was usually a rickshaw pedalled by a muscular young man. For slightly longer trips, this was an ancient vehicle reeking of unfamiliar tobacco and body odors. For truly distant destinations, we traveled by train, often for several days at a time.

I can no more describe the colors and incredible variety of India than I can paint in words the splendor of a prairie sunset or the monumentality of the Canadian Rockies. Some scenes will remain permanently imprinted upon the fabric of my being. Scenes from the train, including open fields dotted with agricultural workers squatting in the early dawn to defecate. Scenes in railway stations where cows often stumbled about amidst the local vendors from whom we purchased food at various stops. Sidewalk scenes, including a lovely young girl combing her raven tresses while peering into a tiny mirror hung on the large cardboard carton that constituted the walls of her family home. Busy roadways where camels and cars, oxen and trucks, brightly painted buses and taxis, even an occasional elephant juggled for position. A raucous cacophony of sounds amid the crazy-quilt of tableaux in motion.

Not a day passed without a heartrending sight or experience. I'm glad I saw the Taj Mahal, but ultimately, its incredible beauty moved me less than Mother Teresa's Calcutta hospice where I stood transfixed by a glimpse of row upon row of cots, each filled with the dying. It was one of several times that I found myself leaning against the nearest wall, weeping helplessly.

Another example: "We feed ten thousand impoverished people a day" said a young man soliciting for rupees near a long snake of people waiting in line for food. Many who waited their turn were blind, and some had only one arm or one leg. A few had neither arms nor legs, only stumps. I had thought it an exaggeration when, in his novel *A Fine Balance*, Rohinton Mistry described the joy of the quadriplegic who had been given a skateboard by the beggarmaster, a fictional character who gave his charges lessons in appearing pathetic and in eliciting extra handouts from passersby. Now, as I stood looking at the long queue of the hungry and the dispossessed, I felt a tugging at my knees. I looked down to see... a quadriplegic on a skateboard.

Another time, I followed a young man resplendent in white tunic and turban who sat proudly astride a frisky white steed. When he entered a private park, I stopped at the gate. The gatekeeper quickly beckoned to me. "Please come to the wedding. It will be our honor to have you as our guest," he said. Within moments, I was surrounded by friendly people asking me to join them at tables groaning with platters of exotic food and jugs of fruit-topped beverages. Elsewhere, people beckoned me to dance with them in front of bandstands whose irresistible music invited movement.

I was especially drawn to demonstrations of what I assumed was advanced yoga. A little girl that I had spotted earlier running about in a crimson velvet dress was now seated upon the extended arm of a woman — an arm that the woman extended straight out at shoulder height. Not in the slightest did that arm tremble under its load. Unbelieving, I ventured closer to assure myself that the woman was as real as the girl. I stood close enough to see her and to smell her perfume. I could have touched her. I could also have touched a man at a nearby tent who was sitting cross-legged a good twelve inches above the ground. Unbelieving, I walked behind him in search of hidden strings or props, but he clearly had nothing but a column of air beneath his buttocks.

My experiences in India bear out the truth of Mark Twain's words that constitute the epigraph to this chapter:

> Twenty years from now you will be more disappointed by the things you didn't do. So throw off the bowlines. Sail away from the safe harbor. Catch the trade wind in your sails. Explore. Dream. Discover.

Among the many positive aspects of aging is the fact that we are given many opportunities to explore, dream, and discover. During our working life, we sometimes "go on holiday" because a change of routine has become a desperate necessity. Often, the easiest "all-inclusive" seems like the perfect solution. However, after we retire, many of us choose to travel, an activity that I view as very different from merely "vacationing." Here's what one elder emailed when I asked him why he travels so often.

> After travelling, I have moved from seeing difference to seeing similarities. Travel has changed my beliefs about my own country compared to others, often in a surprising way. From "The Canadian Way is the best/only right/good way," to "Maybe the way in Otherlandestan makes more sense." Travel has also led to other changes. I've learned to cycle or walk instead of taking the car and rushing about. Sometimes, I just stop, sit at a cafe, and do some people watching. It leads me to wonder why some folks seek out the familiar (hotel chains, etc.) while others seek out the unexpected. For me, walking in the footsteps of the greats (Caesar, Churchill) and in the footsteps of the humble (my grandfather's home in rural Australia) has brought about a mental shift that I welcome. Travel brings me fresh perspectives that greatly enhance my life.

When actual travel is precluded, there are many ways to experience its benefits without ever leaving home. Next week, I anticipate attending a Hindu baby-naming ceremony to which I have been invited. Last week, I was invited for dinner at the home of a Muslim family from Pakistan. Being at their table, sharing our limited knowledge of one another's culture, these to me are opportunities for much more than just personal enjoyment or emotional enrichment. They are occasions where it is possible to create a gram of kindness in a world where political and regional and religious differences tend to divide rather than link. I never fail to feel uplifted by experiencing our common humanity writ large. When I can no longer travel, I hope I will still reach out to people from other lands as graciously as people elsewhere have reached out to me.

———∿∿———

IDEA:

> Travel lures us to explore and to embrace difference. Difference in landscape, in language, and in culture. Kind people, interesting people, and different people can also be found here at home.

ACTION:

1. Travel often carries a high environmental cost including CO_2 emissions from flying and waste creation. How might you travel with a lighter footprint? Think about avoiding single-use plastic items like straws, plastic bags, water bottles, and cutlery. Consider flying less frequently or embracing "slow travel."

2. Think about ways to make deeper local connections such as avoiding pre-packaged vacations and cruises; staying with a local family or a family-owned guesthouse; taking a language course; shopping at local markets, restaurants, and shops; or volunteering at a school or a gathering place where you are likely to meet people from other lands.

3. Consider more deeply your interest in far-off places. Are you traveling just to have something to do, or because you are genuinely interested in another country? Research how you might engage with those interests and with people from other countries when you travel rather than simply "consuming" the destination.

4. Invite someone from another culture to celebrate one of your holidays. Attend a public event that commemorates an occasion that is not part of your own tradition.

Shedding Cultural Baggage

*When we harbor negative emotions toward
others or toward ourselves... we poison our
own physical and spiritual systems. By far
the strongest poison to the human spirit is
the inability to forgive oneself or another
person.*

— Carolyn Myss, *Anatomy of the Spirit* (1996)

C HINA, INDIA, these were countries I was eager to experience, but
Berlin was a destination I dreaded. Despite having previously cultivated close friendships with a handful of Germans, I still carried lots
of internal baggage, all of it heavy.

Most people have someone or something they'd prefer to forget.
Some people need to forgive long-buried parents who failed to shield
and nurture them. Some people need to forgive living members of
their family who persistently disappointed them. Others need to forgive former friends or business partners who betrayed them. I needed
to forgive an entire nation.

I went to Berlin to launch the German translation of *Letters from
the Lost: A Memoir of Discovery*. The "discovery" had included many
facts that I had not known about the fate of my family in the Nazi era.
My route to the venue where I was scheduled to speak, the imposing
German Historical Museum, took me past the Reichstag.

I had seen the steps of the Reichstag before, in the black-and-white
newsreels of my childhood. I remember seeing a ranting, mustachioed
Hitler standing atop those steps, spewing his hatred. I was grateful

that my publisher had thought to wait at the museum entrance, for my legs were trembling as I mounted the staircase and crossed the vast marble lobby to reach the amphitheatre where I was to address a German audience.

In Berlin, forgetting is impossible. Over the years, Germany has made remembering an art as well as an official policy. Germany tells the world that it is only by remembering the past that we have any likelihood of avoiding similar mistakes in the future. The reminders are unavoidable. In Berlin, history is omnipresent. Even the sidewalks are studded with *Stolpersteine*, raised stumbling blocks inscribed with the names of Jews who once lived in the adjacent buildings.

After my speech, I fled to the Berlin train station hours before departure time, eager to escape the barrage of reminders. Today I know that it was not from Berlin that I longed to escape, but from my own need to overcome a lifelong habit of recoiling from all things German.

And yet, in town after town, in city after city, I spoke. In churches and auditoriums from one end of the country to the other, I spoke to Germans who had wrestled with their own past. Most were the children and grandchildren of Nazis who, to some extent, had countenanced the destruction of Jews. At the very least, by their inaction and their silence, those parents and grandparents had paved the way for the extermination of my family.

Some Germans wept as they listened to my words. Many asked penetrating questions. A few bought my book by the armload, vowing to give one to each member of the family to ensure that history would never repeat itself.

What left indelible traces on my heart were the thousands of students I had been invited to address. I had expected to speak to individual classes, but instead, I faced entire auditoriums filled with young people. Each day, a new school with a new committee of teachers and administrators reaching out with a welcoming handshake. Each day, I became more comfortable with my audience, while remaining surprised by their openness and willingness to listen.

Never had I experienced such total attention. I spoke in two-hour slots, usually from 10 a.m. to noon. Despite the autumn sunshine beaming through the windows, the students listened. Their tummies may have rumbled in anticipation of lunch, their limbs may have longed to stretch, but instead, they sat. They listened and they heard.

After my speech, one of the teachers usually read a few passages from the book. Unfailingly, these readings were met with rapt attention. Afterwards, it was question period. Inevitably, I was struck by the insight these questions reflected.

In one school, a teacher read aloud this passage from one of my Uncle Arnold's letters. It describes his experience of being dehumanized:

> The Germans followed the principle of not doing anything to us themselves. Instead, they trained the Czechs in anti-Semitism, and in this, they succeeded very well. For our first horrendous surprise, they picked Yom Kippur, the holiest of days on the Jewish calendar, to make us turn in all radios and report the precise value of all monetary and personal possessions.
>
> Blow upon blow followed, usually at two-week intervals. Always something new, something else that was forbidden, a new limitation that made our life difficult, until bit by bit, life became impossible. After the radios, it was musical instruments, tools, trunks and suitcases, ski equipment, woolen clothing, and underwear if you had more than two sets. Even the poor animals weren't exempt. All dogs and cats and canaries had to be taken to the collection depot.

Was wollte die Wehrmacht mit den Kanarienvögel? asked one young boy. "Why did the military need pet canaries?" I scarcely needed to answer, for no sooner had he voiced his question than the penny dropped for him, and for everyone in the auditorium. The army didn't need aging dogs, cats, or canaries. Asking people to give up a beloved pet was sheer malice, just another way to speed up the dehumanization process that culminated in Jews being disposable entities, known only by the numbers tattooed on their arms.

The penny also dropped for me. Today, we no longer tattoo numbers on people's arms, but not so long ago, in my lifetime, right here in Canada, we also dehumanized people in abhorrent ways. Recently, I attended a book reading by Bev Sellars, former chief of the Xat'sull First Nation and author of *They Called Me Number One*. The author spent her childhood in a church-run residential school whose aim was to "civilize" Indigenous children. She tells of hunger, forced labor, and physical beatings with leather straps. She tells of children confined and denigrated for the crime of not being white or Christian. To me, most shocking of all was the fact that each child was given a number. Hers was Number One.

If we are to look ourselves in the mirror and feel good about who we are, elderhood demands that we acknowledge whatever pain was inflicted upon us, along with whatever pain we may have inflicted upon others, either personally or culturally. It demands that we refuse to divorce ourselves from the society in which we live, and that we accept responsibility, as did the Germans who attended my talks. They came to acknowledge and to learn more about what their ancestors had done — or failed to do while there was still time to protest. They are a new generation, these Germans, and they could have spent their time much more pleasantly elsewhere, and yet, they came to hear me speak.

It led me to wonder how much progress we had made in North America toward acknowledging the harm inflicted by our ancestors and by earlier governments. Unlike Germany, we have no *Stolpersteine* and relatively few markers to indicate where Indigenous people lived prior to being removed to "reservations." In our eagerness to celebrate the Canada of today, we hurry past unpalatable realities including the Chinese head tax and Canada's refusal to allow the *Komagata Maru* or the *St. Louis* to land, lest the frightened refugees aboard taint the nation.

A musical moment in a German school lingers in my memory. It was after the formal program had ended, after I had been thanked and presented with a bouquet, after most of the students had filed out of the auditorium. As so often before, a few students came on stage to talk privately with me and to ask questions in a less public fashion. Suddenly, I heard music. It was Leonard Cohen's "Hallelujah." The song emanated from a girl with a harp.

I had not noticed her when she entered the auditorium, and I only looked up when she began to play. It gave me goosebumps, that Hallelujah, for it expresses much that cannot be spoken. We sometimes sing it in my synagogue in an effort to reach beyond concrete meaning. Hearing the familiar melody but with the words in German was doubly disorienting. Emotion overwhelmed me. Somehow, I stumbled off the stage and stood speechless before her. With every fiber of my being, I listened. When the music stopped, I hugged her speechlessly, for no words could express my feelings. Even now, I shiver as the intensity of the moment engulfs me like an incoming tide.

The song is a symbol for me of human outreach and of human commonality. What binds us to our fellow humans is so much stronger than that which separates us. As we age, we need to allow the healing waters of forgiveness and reconciliation to wash away our own pain along with the tears of other individuals and communities. For our own sake, with every passing year, letting go of old hatreds and animosities becomes more important. Martin Luther King Jr. got it right: "Darkness cannot drive out darkness; only light can do that. Hate cannot drive out hate; only love can do that."

—∿∿—

IDEA:

> My trip to Germany to introduce Germans to a book describing how inhumane they had been to my family and to six million other Jews was an eye-opener. When I saw how much Germans had done to atone for their

actions under Hitler's leadership, how much they were still doing to ensure that this generation and future generations would learn from the errors of their ancestors, I let go of my own negative attitude toward Germany and its inhabitants.

Are there things we can learn from Germany? How shall we accept responsibility for pain inflicted on others in North America, including pain inflicted by political leaders on our behalf?

ACTION:

1. Do you carry with you an attitude toward some group that is weighing you down? After a Rottweiler snarled at you, did you simply start avoiding that particular dog? Or have you spent a lifetime afraid of dogs?

2. Have you forgiven yourself for unintentional errors and mistakes? Ultimately, self-compassion allows us to see others through a more compassionate lens.

3. Has someone harmed you? Consider writing a letter to that person, a letter in which you forgive in order to lighten your own load. Decide whether you want to send the letter or whether the mere act of writing is enough. Remind yourself of what Mahatma Gandhi said: *The weak can never forgive. Forgiveness is the attribute of the strong.*

4. Identify the trauma whose impact you no longer want to carry. Acknowledge the pain inflicted upon you, knowing that if you fail to do so, you not only carry a heavy load, but you may also be inclined to dismiss the suffering of others. Write about the trauma on a piece of paper, and then, light a candle. Slowly and ceremoniously, burn the paper.

Finding Balance and Hope

I have seen no more evident monstrosity
and miracle in the world than myself.

— Montaigne

L ETTING GO OF OLD ANIMOSITIES IS HARD, but as we age, it is an essential step on the path to reconciliation and inner peace. Navigating life when one is a member of a minority group is doubly difficult, but age at least provides some perspective and some hand-holds when the boat is rocking.

Last November, in preparation for a Remembrance Day ceremony at which I'd been asked to speak, I picked up Alex Kershaw's *The Liberator*, a book that describes the exploits of an American soldier in the Second World War. It contains a chapter on the liberation of Dachau.

> The Americans came across a courtyard with a puzzling array of vertical poles. Penned up beside it were over 100 large dogs — Alsatians, Dobermans, Great Danes ... trained to attack inmates ... A guard explained: "We made prisoners strip at gunpoint and tied them to the poles. Then, we tapped the victims' testicles with sticks and urged the dogs to jump up and rip them off. When the victims had been neutered, we used to roar with laughter and reward our hounds with red meat."[3]

My Uncle Emil died in Dachau. I dare not think of how he met his end. Uncle Emil, to whom I owe my life. He saw the writing on the wall, and he urged my father to flee. My father didn't want to leave his aging parents, his brothers and his sisters and their young families. He loved his world. It was the only world he had ever known or wanted. Uncle Emil insisted.

Uncle Emil's daughter Ilserl was my favorite cousin and playmate. I've been told that we were inseparable back then. Several of the letters sent to my father after we reached Canada contain messages addressed to me in her childish script.

I am haunted by how Ilserl would have met her death. Like other children in Auschwitz, hand-in-hand with her mother and her two-year-old sister, Ilserl would have walked at gunpoint to the building where they were stripped of their clothing, then sent naked into the gas chamber. I have read that death in a gas chamber was seldom instant. The clawmarks on the walls indicate how desperately people tried to climb toward life-giving air. A guard would watch through a peephole. Finally, when all was still, the guard would announce that it was safe to go in. Only then would men in gas masks enter with pitchforks, ready to gather up the naked bodies and take them to the crematorium for mass burning.

It would be easy for me to move from such thoughts to the belief that humans are a bad lot. I could easily conclude that people are so eager to obey the dictates of their leaders and peers that they can be brainwashed into beast-like behavior. I was shocked — and yet not surprised — during a recent election to hear a respected political commentator say that despite all the lip-service paid to our democracies, people don't like making decisions and will vote for the father figure who tells them how to think and what to do.

It would certainly be all too easy for me to distrust, and to live in a state of perpetual watchfulness. The daily headlines scream out to me that soon, in their latest reincarnation, the Cossacks will be coming. Sometimes, I imagine that already, I can hear their marching footsteps. But constant stress is not a good state in which to dwell, which is why, as an elder, I consciously choose to let go of the negative, and to seek out reasons for hope.

It may be scraping the bottom of the barrel, but I take comfort in knowing that even killing must be learned.

> During the first try, my hand trembled a bit as I shot, but one gets used to it. By the tenth try I aimed calmly and shot surely at the many women, children, and infants ... Infants flew in great arcs through the air, and we shot them to pieces in flight.[4]

I also take comfort from knowing that many soldiers in the First World War actually fired above the heads of the enemy because they could not look another human in the eye and shoot. Perhaps some actions are so inhumane that they break us.

Not long ago, I had lengthy conversations with a former soldier now suffering from PTSD. He came regularly to the dinners for those in need of food and human comfort that we (a group of volunteers) prepared at a church in my neighborhood. Despite his military bearing, this former soldier was such a gentle man — kind, sensitive, and caring. His suffering touched me deeply. He could not forgive himself for harm inflicted while obeying orders and while executing actions as commanded by his superior officers. For me, his pain was proof that most humans have a conscience, and that people want to do what is right and good.

I call this hope, and I firmly believe that hope is not something that you have or don't have. Hope is a choice that you make. I often repeat to myself Emily Dickinson's poetic words:

> "Hope" is the thing with feathers
> That perches in the soul
> And sings the tune without the words
> And never stops — at all.[5]

I choose to believe that humans evolve in more than just physical form. I choose to believe that although genuine progress may appear painfully slow, it does occur. Finally, I choose to believe that progress will occur in time to prevent or limit whatever unthinkable acts lie dormant but possible.

For me, and for humans everywhere, hope is as essential as the air we breathe. Without hope, what would be the point of living?

As an undergraduate, I was drawn to existential nihilism, and eagerly argued that life is without intrinsic meaning, purpose, or value. I spouted Nietzschean aphorisms and devoured every written word of Sartre and Camus. I refused to see life as other than absurd.

No longer. Age and life itself have changed me. Today, I scoff at those who peddle nihilism, whether as a philosophy or as an attitude. Now, I scorn statements that might have fallen from my own lips sixty years ago.

> I don't care what anyone says or how often or how winningly they say it: no one will ever, ever be able to persuade me that life is some awesome, rewarding treat. Because, here's the truth: life is catastrophe ... better never [to be] born into this cesspool. Sinkhole of hospital beds, coffins, and broken hearts. No release, no appeal ... no way forward but age and loss, and no way out but death.[6]

Daily, I seek out the hopeful, even in its smallest manifestations, to counterbalance the barrage of negativity that assaults us with every new headline. Counterbalancing is as much a psychological necessity as it is a physical one. In order to avoid bone-breaking falls — a serious threat to many seniors, I reach for the balance board at the gym. This piece of equipment, a flat piece of wood resembling a skateboard mounted at the center on a single roller, provides practice in standing steadily on two feet, without wobbling from side to side. This is an outer stance that reflects the inner balance toward which we strive with the passing years.

Around me, I see seniors who are the very opposite of the unbalanced, angry adults who carped and complained as I was growing up. Today's seniors strike me as far kinder, more caring, and far more capable of human connectedness than was true for the seniors I used to know. Perhaps that was because they had so few role models. I think of one dear friend of the family who retired from a challenging career to take up work as his wife's chauffeur. Every week, he could be spotted outside the beauty salon to which she had managed to drive quite happily for many years. He was witty, charming, and brilliant but, in retirement, he lost his balance. Every action seemed pointless; nothing seemed worth doing. I don't know whether today he might be diagnosed as clinically depressed, but I did watch him become a mere shadow of himself.

While I hardly see myself as a role model of equanimity, I do find that age allows me to return more easily to a position of neutrality from which I can shift gears as necessary. That does not keep me from collecting quotes like this one by Václav Havel: "Hope is not the conviction that something will turn out well, but the certainty that something makes sense, regardless of how it turns out."

I'm drawn to philosophers and scientists who see reason to be cautiously hopeful, and to thinkers like primatologist Frans de Waal:

> We humans are complex characters who easily form social hierarchies, yet in fact have an aversion to them ... We walk on two legs: a social and a selfish one. We tolerate differences in status and income only up to a degree, and begin to root for the underdog as soon as this boundary is overstepped. We have a deeply ingrained sense of fairness, which derives from our long history as egalitarians.[7]

I treasure the slender thread of hope that we are all moving closer to one another. I'm delighted wherever I see egalitarianism in action, and barriers breaking down, as at the baby-naming ceremony to which I was recently invited. The mother was East Indian, the father was not, but both were clearly eager to bestow upon their child the customs and traditions of his heritage while demonstrating that love need no longer be limited to members of one's own clan. The young couple and their guests were a perfect reflection of the Canada of tomorrow.

Statistics Canada confirms that inclusivity and cross-cultural connections are no longer unusual.

> Last month, Statistics Canada released its latest numbers on couples who cross racial or ethnic lines, revealing surprising and continued growth. Mixed unions are no longer unusual. ... As such, we're setting the global standard for multicultural acceptance and integration. It is, of course, going too far to claim Canada has completely transcended all forms of prejudice or bigotry. ... But it also implies an underlying respect for choice in personal relationships that transcends other prejudices. In other words, love may one day conquer all.[8]

I need to believe that progress and change for the better are possible, for humanity as well as for me. I need to believe that human aspiration is toward the light, and that compassion and kindness *are* deeply rooted in the human soul. Sometimes, the impulse to care for one another gets warped, but it *does* exist.

Holding on to animosities is a choice. So is hope. As we age, we can live with resentment, or we can let hope be the beacon that beckons us to rise each morning. We can embrace hope because it animates our efforts to engage with and to improve the world. Elders know that even when dark clouds obscure the sun, hope summons us to look for the light.

—·∿∿·—

IDEA:

> Balance means neither being a Cassandra nor playing ostrich. When you hold despair in your left hand, reach for hope with the right hand. With your balance thus restored, you will envision solutions, and you will want to act to improve the situation.

ACTION:

1. Read through some negative/tragic newspaper articles and envision a better outcome. How might you take some action, no matter how small, to help make this "hope" real?

2. List the people and their actions that offer you a glimpse of blue sky beyond the gathering clouds.

3. Limit your exposure to the daily news for a while. After a few days, take stock. Is your head full of armed criminals, politicians making terrible decisions, powerful people lining their pockets, the greedy taking advantage of the dispossessed, of environmental degradation and disaster? Or have your thoughts turned toward more positive scenarios, including good people and their actions?

4. Delve more deeply into how you can find and spread hope by reading *Intrinsic Hope: Living Courageously in Troubled Times* by Kate Davies.

Delving Deeper

No Easy Answers

Justice will not be served until those
who are unaffected are as outraged
as those who are.

— Benjamin Franklin

A T EIGHTY, I wrestle with issues as seriously as I did in my twenties when university opened up new worlds for me. For me, to be alive is to think as well as to feel. The fact that there may be no answers, or at least no easy ones, does not absolve me from the need to think. Nor does it eliminate the desire to do so. Thinking is not easy, but age is not a "Get Out of Jail Free" card.

A friend recently sent the following email.

> I love the interesting and insightful discussions that we
> contemplate together. It offers us good perspectives even
> though the questions we ask never seem to have simple,
> obvious answers.

The previous day we had discussed borders, and whether it is morally defensible to tell people to "keep out" no matter what is happening in their country of birth. In what now seems like "once upon a time," the US engraved these well-known words by Emma Lazarus on a plaque inside the pedestal of the Statue of Liberty:

> Give me your tired, your poor,
> Your huddled masses yearning to breathe free
> The wretched refuse of your teeming shore.
> Send these, the homeless, tempest-tost to me...

Our discussion had touched on whether these words still apply in the US or anywhere else today. We debated whether, when climate change brings drought to a country, those of us living in fertile lands have the right to tell refugees to stay home and starve. We discussed whether, when governments become dictatorships, those living in freedom have the right to tell others to fight and kill until the leadership changes. We asked if those of us living amid prosperity have the right to tell citizens in countries with few natural resources and huge poverty that they lack the entry requirements for "our" country. In her novel *The Poisonwood Bible*, writing from the standpoint of the daughter of missionaries in Central Africa, Barbara Kingsolver asks: "Does anyone deserve to be born in Africa?"

Despite a lifetime of thinking I'd kept up with the news, I shake my head in horror at the degree of my own ignorance of world events. Of Africa, especially, a continent of which I know so little. From my current reading:

> Somalia is familiar with military intervention, from the RAF's bombing in 1920 to Bush Sr.'s intervention in 1992. ... He dispatched tens of thousands of troops to Somalia, tasked with "creating a secure environment for the delivery of humanitarian aid," but the mission ended ... with the deaths of hundreds, probably thousands, of Somali civilians before the hasty withdrawal of US and allied troops in 1994.[1]

What occupied my thoughts so thoroughly in 1994 that it prevented all awareness of the slaughter of innocents? The article I am reading goes on to describe the current situation in the area:

> This vast territory (stretching through the Sahel and across the continent before leaping the Gulf of Aden to Yemen), once the site of fierce resistance to colonial incursions, is now paying a heavy price for the greenhouse gas emissions of the industrialized north.

The article does not dwell on waterless wells and dried up river-beds, or on children dying of cholera and starvation. It describes instead the animal deaths that accompany desertification:

> A black liquid stained the dry red earth. ... Beside it was the carcass of a donkey, white bone showing beneath what little flesh remained. A few metres away, a warthog lay rotting, and beyond that a camel. For miles outside the village ... thousands of sheep and goats lay strewn in various states of decay. The contents of their stomachs, it was easy to see, were mainly colourful shards of plastic ingested in the absence of natural pasture.

Problems to which there are no easy answers, and there may only be partial ones. Perhaps throwing open the doors fully is beyond what even wealthy states can do without bankrupting themselves in the short term. Still, such questions need to be asked in order to trigger long-term thinking about issues of fairness and social justice.

Elders can and should spend time pondering large questions. Because we have firsthand knowledge of the myriad ways that life can be unfair, we must stand with the young, ready to do battle for a world of justice for everyone. We all have the potential to make a positive contribution, and many elders are doing just that.

Here's how Joan Chittister describes the role of the elder:

> Older people have what this world needs most: the kind of experience that can save the next generation from the errors of the one before them. This is a generation, for instance, that knows the unfathomable horrors of mass genocide and holocaust. This generation knows that war does nothing but plant the seeds of the next one. ... The older generation knows that the only thing that is good for any of us in the long run is what is good for all of us.[2]

It is a huge challenge to think about what is good for all of us instead of just focusing on ourselves, or on what may be good for our group or our tribe. In a democracy, we are responsible for thinking about what is best for our nation at the very least, and perhaps for all who dwell on planet earth.

Thinking about what is good for all of us has led a friend in her seventies to devote months to protecting elephants and other threatened forms of wildlife in Africa. Similar thoughts have prompted a newly retired couple to complete teacher training in order to bring literacy to developing countries. Another friend just told me of a travel agency whose expeditions always start with a visit to orphanages and villages where school supplies, sporting equipment, toys, clothing, anything a tourist can collect at home and bring is gratefully received. Still another retiree has been to Guatemala, attempting to bring healing and a sense of self-worth to imprisoned "women" aged thirteen to seventeen.

Fortunately, we need not travel far afield in order to participate in shaping a future that takes into account much more than our own comfort or pleasure. In a book published when he was eighty-four, Erik Erikson points out that elders instinctively seek to preserve and protect.

> Old people are, by nature, conservationists. Long memories and wider perspectives lend urgency to the maintenance of our natural world. Old people, quite understandably, seem to feel more keenly the obstruction of open waterfronts, the cutting of age-old stands of trees, the paving of vast stretches of fertile countryside, and the pollution of once clear streams and lakes. Their longer memories recall the beauty of their surroundings in earlier years. We need those memories and those voices.[3]

As elders whose vivid memories include wars and the suffering they occasioned, we need not and should not idly stand by. We can stay abreast of world events, challenging our politicians and decision-makers to change course when we discover facts like the following:

> Globally, 12 times as much money is invested in fighting each other as in ensuring that children around the world have access to education, primary care, and clean water.[4]
>
> Canada remains among the nations that profit greatly from arms sales. Despite the fact that weapons shipped into Syria and Iraq by Western countries are now in the hands of ISIS and other terrorist groups, headlines in several newspapers in June 2016 crowed that "Canada has soared in global rankings to become the second biggest arms dealer to the Middle East."[5]

Many elders with power of the purse-string have responded to this issue by switching to "ethical" investments. All of us, however, have voting power and the ability to exert political pressure as individuals and through our clubs, churches, and organizations. We can advocate clearly and loudly for peaceful solutions. We can devote time and energy to thinking about what is good for everyone. We can speak out and take action on a wide range of issues. That is as it should be.

I may not be as wise or as brave as I wish, but is anyone? What I do know is that only by thinking deeply and honestly about my values will I become an elder who respects the face in the mirror, regardless of the number of wrinkles etched upon it. Regardless of age, the people I know and love are all seeking to do whatever they can in a complex world where there are few easy answers. In doing so, they bring good to themselves and to others. Their feelings of self-worth grow accordingly, and they are experiencing their life as rich, full, and rewarding.

In an earlier chapter, I quoted the ADA motto "Hope is not a plan." If I reject hope, then I condemn myself to living in despair, spending the next precious part of the only life of which I can be certain grumbling and pining for the way things used to be before "they" (choose whatever group you most despise to label as "they") ruined everything. Option B would be to spend every waking moment of every day distracting myself with so-called pleasures (or the planning and anticipation of such pleasures.) In this way, I could assure that my mind is never burdened with anything more problematic that solving the daily sudoku.

I have chosen Option C. This means that I have no right to expect others to effect change if I am unwilling to even try to do my best in my remaining years. Of course, there is nothing that I, single-handedly can do, but as we used to say back when we sang *The Dawning of the Age of Aquarius*: "If you are not a part of the solution, you are part of the problem."

—◦◦◦—

IDEA:

> Just because you're old doesn't mean it's time to stop thinking. Life is not a game of Monopoly, and age is not a "Get Out of Jail Free" card.

ACTION:

1. Advocate clearly and loudly for peaceful solutions to global issues, or work locally to effect change.

2. Apply the professional expertise that you have garnered during your years in the workforce to effect change. Inspire others to put their shoulder to the wheel.

3. Develop new skills and insights that will enable you to contribute more effectively toward creating the world of your dreams.

4. Think of how you'd like to be remembered and the legacy you'd like to leave. Will that be more than a pile of possessions?

Possible starting points

1. Switch your investments to ethical investments, start an ethical investing club, or pool money with others to

provide "angel" investment funds for social enterprises. Check out some relevant books, e.g. *Invest Like You Give a Damn: Make Money, Change the World, Sleep Well at Night* (Marc de Sousa-Shields) or *The Clean Money Revolution: Reinventing Power, Purpose, and Capitalism* (Joel Solomon).

2. Join or volunteer with a progressive political party and help mobilize progressive votes in the next election

3. Find an organization or a nonprofit with progressive goals, be it wilderness protection, poverty reduction, housing, or another cause, and volunteer. Good starting points for Canadians include www.ashoka.org whose stated mission is "to shape a global, entrepreneurial, competitive citizen sector: one that allows social entrepreneurs to thrive and enables the world's citizens to think and act as changemakers." Americans will find a multitude of volunteer opportunities via www.usa.gov/volunteer.

4. Start your own activist group to speak out or initiate action on any issue, be it climate change, local transport, food sharing, food security, gardening, etc. An excellent resource would be *Changemakers: Embracing Hope, Taking Action, and Transforming the World* (Fay Weller and Mary Wilson).

Who Are You?

Doubt is an unpleasant sensation,
but certainty is absurd.

— Voltaire

VOLTAIRE'S CLAIM THAT WE ARE UNCOMFORTABLE with uncertainty is everywhere in evidence. It astounds me how often people stop in mid-conversation to look up answers on their cell phones. Who was that movie actor? When did he die? Where is he buried? What is the population of Moose Jaw? The greater our access to the facts, the more we seem unsettled by uncertainty.

Does certainty exist? Do we even know ourselves with certainty? In what ways can we be relied upon? Will we always step up to the plate? When will our fears, doubts, and hesitations kick in? To such questions, the internet provides no answers. For elders, the seemingly simplest question is often the hardest to answer. At some point, perhaps on some long, sleepless night, each of us must ask "Who am I?"

Psychiatrist Kevin Solomons notes how seldom people introduce themselves or even think of themselves beyond their social roles.

> They're a teacher, a mother, an uncle, a CEO, a professor, a daughter, a brother and so on. People seldom think to answer the question of who they are in the ways ... of who they need to be.[6]

Do we vanish beyond our roles? And how can I know who I need to be? What constitutes my identity? Does that change when the circumstances themselves change? Moments ago, I received an email from a friend whose mother has just been moved from hospital to hospice. It reads in part "We are praying, praying, and praying that she goes as soon as possible. So sad. I love her very much." In addition to being sad, will my friend be different after she is stripped of the role of daughter? Or does she, like her mother, have an essence beyond her social identity, an inner flame that death alone can extinguish?

Are we not born who we are, as I see again and again in my grandchildren? One child is strong-willed, eager to grab life by the horns, and ready to surmount every obstacle. A second child is introspective, weighing all matters carefully, and only rarely exceeding the reasoned and reasonable. A third child is born outgoing and confident, certain that the world awaits, and that no target is beyond reach. A fourth is surprisingly sensitive and wise at a tender age. To each child, I say "Bravo! You need to be exactly who you are, and I will always love you for it."

Greatly as I love and cherish my children and grandchildren, still, they are not, and they cannot be the justification of my existence. They are small miracles, born who they are, and only minimally shaped by my influence. I see many aspects of myself reflected in them, and yet, none of myself in their core being.

Some people do view their offspring as the justification of their life. They see themselves as having existed only to pass on their genes. In no way can I see my family in such a light. They were born thanks to a force and a process and a blending of coincidence that is mathematically beyond my ability to calculate or conceptualize. My life is mine, their lives are theirs, to shape according to their inner gifts, their inborn nature and their deepest longings.

However, if neither my family nor my former profession define who I am, then who am I? And more importantly, how is this reflected in my life?

Am I merely a product of my culture and environment? Besides, what is a culture? Specifically, what is my culture? Does growing up in Canada with a legal document suffice to make me Canadian? Am I different in any meaningful way from Canadians whose parents spoke Italian or Greek or Mandarin or English? What meaning shall I attach to my fondness for the taste of *Knödel* and *Kraut*, or to the fact that I prefer *Apfelstrudel* to apple pie? I used to envy classmates who wore pleated skirts and proudly advertised their Scottish heritage through the tartan they wore. I'm not sure I can imagine feeling connected to a clan. Even in the company of fellow Jews, I often feel my separateness and my difference as greatly as whatever commonalities we may share. The deeper I probe, the more the answers elude me.

In search of an identity, I have tried on several hats, none of which seem to fit. For some Canadians, regionality is a distinguishing feature, but that does not work for me. I am not like friends who grew up on the prairies, nor like loyal Newfoundlanders with seafaring roots, let alone like certain Québécois who consider themselves *pure laine*. Despite my unquestioned loyalty to Canada, my abiding love for Her Majesty (long may she reign!), and my deep respect for the parliamentary traditions that have come to us from across the sea, I remain conscious of the fact that I'm not a daughter of the Anglo-French Christian founders of our nation.

My pride in Canada is inextricably linked to the gradual inclusivity that is still in the process of evolving. To a greater degree than most countries, we have become a cultural mosaic that welcomes diversity and difference. At the same time, I remain sharply conscious of the many forms of racism and exclusion that exist now and that are a feature of our history as a nation.

But even these abstractions failed to help me answer the question "Who am I?" I soon found it impossible to say who I was without delving further into my roots and my own history. Alas, the more I took stock, the more aware I became of difference.

This was definitely not a direction in which I wanted to go. For many years, I had considered the focus on difference to be what divides people. All too often, difference leads one group to feel superior to another. And yet, there the issue stood, boulder-like, blocking my path to inner growth. How could I develop and strengthen my core self without a clear idea that self? What is this amorphous essence called "self" that lies beyond culture, yet bears its stamp?

I often wonder how some Indigenous individuals and bands have moved so successfully beyond the hurtful labels attached to them. How did they avoid being poisoned by negative stereotyping and the paralysis it engenders? Perhaps they listened to the call of the drum instead of to the disparaging voices of white settlers. Perhaps, intuitively, they knew that whatever we pay attention to becomes stronger.

> If you constantly think about what frightens you, you will become more fearful. If you constantly think about how unfair life is, you will see more and more around you to support this point of view ... If you believe your life is worthless, your choices and behavior will reflect that.[7]

I applaud those who sidestep bullying voices that plant seeds of self-doubt. The latter is a force with debilitating power, and I often crumble under its mighty weight. At such times, the Helen who lives independently, thinks deeply, and acts compassionately vanishes. My mirror reflects only a woebegone weakling who knows nothing and does even less. The fluctuation in my own self-perception leads me to seek out evidence that we are all in the same boat, and that we all "express a personality inevitably double, and full of the tensions and contradictions that touch any real life."[8]

My favourite example of a real life of acknowledged contradictions is Dietrich Bonhoeffer, the German pastor who opposed Hitler's euthanasia program. Bonhoeffer's poem "Who Am I?" was written in prison shortly before his execution in 1945 at Flossenbürg concentration camp.

> Who am I? They often tell me
> I stepped from my cell's confinement
> Calmly, cheerfully, firmly,
> Like a Squire from his country house.

Who am I? They often tell me
I used to speak to my warders
Freely and friendly and clearly,
As though it were mine to command.

Who am I? They also tell me
I bore the days of misfortune
Equably, smilingly, proudly,
Like one accustomed to win.

Am I then really that which other men tell of?
Or am I only what I myself know of myself?
Restless and longing and sick, like a bird in a cage,
Struggling for breath, as though hands were
    compressing my throat,
Yearning for colors, for flowers, for the voices of birds,
Thirsting for words of kindness, for neighborliness,
Tossing in expectations of great events,
Powerlessly trembling for friends at an infinite distance,
Weary and empty at praying, at thinking, at making,
Faint, and ready to say farewell to it all.

Who am I? This or the Other?
Am I one person today and tomorrow another?
Am I both at once? A hypocrite before others,
And before myself a contemptible woebegone weakling?
Or is something within me still like a beaten army
Fleeing in disorder from victory already achieved?

Who am I? They mock me, these lonely questions
    of mine.
Whoever I am, Thou knowest, O God, I am thine!

Bonhoeffer found his answer in God, but the question has forced me and other elders to rethink previously unexamined assumptions. Is there a constancy and a consistency to the self that does not fluctuate? Do we always recognize the face in the mirror? I recall scratching my head in high school upon encountering the so-called wisdom of Polonius who counsels his son "This above all, to thine own self be true." At the time, I saw myself as having multiple selves, each of which I experienced as genuine. Although age has erased some of the extremes, I am still not totally singular. Is anyone fixed and unvarying?

Besides, are any of us capable of seeing the big picture? Are we all akin to Bonhoeffer's army of soldiers, fleeing in disorder from the chaos of battle? Does our limited perspective obscure the fact that elsewhere, there has been a decisive victory? We are so rarely aware of more than one thing at a time, and so often, we see ourselves as one way or the other instead of as both strong and weak, both ____ and ____.

***

Recently, on a dreary day of rain, I forced myself to step out of the house. As I opened my umbrella, a glimpse of sunshine caught my eye. Immediately I detoured via the park in hopes of finding a rainbow. As so often before, I stood awestruck as bands of color arched across the sky, creating a spectacle that never fails to excite me. Behind me, cars rushed to their destinations. In front of me, a group of boys had eyes only for the trajectory of a soccer ball. I felt alone in noticing the miracle of a rainbow.

Like the rainbow, we are all miniscule ribbons of constantly fluctuating color, yet together, our commonalities form an arc of astonishing beauty.

— "Who am I?"

— That depends on which day you ask.

— Do I have an essence that exists beyond my physical, professional, and relational attributes?

— I think so.

— Am I more than the sum total of my achievements?

— I hope so.

— Am I more than a collection of qualities?

— Maybe.

— Do I exist beyond the quick flash of thoughts and feelings?

— Possibly.

— Is anything about me certain?

— Perhaps.

— When called upon, can I be relied upon?

— Probably.

— Would I step up to the plate if asked to sacrifice? Hmmmm.

Such questions and many more continue to haunt me as I age. I am far from alone in having concluded that humans are not cows, and that few of us discover contentment by grazing in green pastures. Our innate longings take us beyond the physical, urging us to use our fullest capacities. As we stretch to reach beyond ourselves, we discover that we can be more than we were even as we are becoming less in other ways.

The more disturbed I get by unanswered questions, the more likely I am to reach for a book to point me in the right direction. Jonathan Sacks has often been my guide.

> Just as every life has a task, so every day brings an opportunity. ... I found the best way of knowing what it is, is to turn the situation upside down. ... There were times when, in crisis, I would await the reassuring word from a friend, until I suddenly saw that I should be the one giving reassurance. The discovery changed my life. That was when I knew that we experience pain to sensitize us to the pain of others. Turning our emotions outward, we can use them as the key to free someone else from the locked room of suffering or disappointment or grief.[9]

When doubt, and especially self-doubt threatens to derail me, I try to follow Sacks' advice by turning the situation upside down. I seek the key that will free someone else from the locked room of his/her suffering, disappointment, or grief. It always helps me, even when I fail to rescue the other.

—∿∿—

IDEA:

> Consistency is rare. Most of us are a blend of qualities and traits, strengths and weaknesses. Assessing who we are and how we are is an essential task of elderhood. Only then can we move forward with clarity and assurance that we are on the right path.

ACTION:

1. Do you vacillate between extremes? Can you identify the people or the situations that tend to trigger these extremes?

2. List the attributes that constitute your identity. Star the ones you like.

3. Jonathan Sacks claims that "Just as every life has a task, so every day brings an opportunity. ... I found the best way of knowing what it is, is to turn the situation upside down." Is there a situation that you could turn upside down in order to be true to who you really are?

4. List three personal attributes that you ascribe to your cultural background. List three more that you consider innate and integral to your persona, your essence, and your soul.

Spiritual Speculation

When I consider how my light is spent
Ere half my days, in this dark world and wide,
And that one Talent which is death to hide,
Lodg'd with me useless, though my Soul more
*   bent*
To serve therewith my Maker, and present
My true account.

OVER THE YEARS, I have frequently given silent thanks to the high school English teacher who made us memorize the above lines from John Milton's poem "On His Blindness."

How to present our true account to our Maker, how to use those decades ahead, these are questions that become particularly relevant to the thinking elder. Does each of us have a single talent? Or, unlike the great poet Milton, does each of us have numerous talents that lie dormant but need to be awakened before we die? Does failing to do so represent a kind of spiritual death and the waste of a good life?

Beyond these lie even more problematic questions: "Are there pearly gates where we will have to pass muster? Is there a Maker who will demand credentials for entry to Paradise? Will we be asked to justify our existence? Does it matter whether we made the most of the gifts we were given?"

For most of my life I was quite happy to dismiss all religion as superstition, as a crutch for people who fail to reach beyond simple answers to complex problems. Aging, and what I see as maturing, has led me to a new humility and to the necessity of revising that opinion.

Now I believe that by whatever scientific principles the universe was created, it exists for a purpose. I believe that each human being has a role to play in that purpose, just as does every tree and bush and shrub. It may be childlike to conceive of the Creator as a Divine Being, to imagine it all beginning with a father figure in idealized human form, but it is as far as my limited brain will stretch. It is no easier for me to believe instead that something comes from nothing, or that the Big Bang simply banged itself in order to produce a cosmos with at least one hundred billion galaxies, a figure that stands only for the *currently humanly observable* universe.

Nor is it easy for me to conceptualize that the human body is made up of 15 trillion cells by volume but an estimated 70 trillion by weight. Even today's *New York Times'* headline news is far beyond my reach: "A team of scientists announced that they had heard and recorded the sound of two black holes colliding *a billion light-years away*, a fleeting chirp that fulfilled the last prediction of Einstein's general theory of relativity."[10]

Because I cannot know, I choose to believe that the universe is a place that far surpasses whatever the neurotransmitters and axons and synapses in my brain can process. The laws of the universe are complex and orderly, and nothing appears pointless or purposeless. Why, then, should we humans alone be purposeless creatures, and why should our actions alone be meaningless?

I choose to think of myself and of all humans as God's right hand, here to create and invent and foster growth in the garden that surrounds us. I know full well that bad things happen to good people, but good things also happen. I choose to believe in the good. I even choose to believe that good people outnumber those we label as evil, and that most of us strive to become better people. I choose to thank God daily for granting me these additional years so that I may grow and be of service.

One of my favourite quotes is from Albert Einstein:

> A hundred times every day, I remind myself that my inner
> and outer life depend on the labors of other men, living and
> dead, and that I must exert myself in order to give in the
> same measure as I have received and am still receiving.[11]

Despite my absolute faith in scientific progress and in education as a tool for human advancement, despite a lifetime of distancing myself from religion, I began to wonder why my ancestors had been part of a belief system that had endured for five thousand years. If brilliant thinkers ranging from Maimonides to Einstein had found their religion relevant, surely I should at least explore the topic.

And so began a spiritual development that in some ways has outdistanced the physical and mental growth inherent in my post-retirement journey. I still don't envision encountering Big-Daddy-in-the-Sky with a winged angel at his side, ready to scoop out my soul and weigh it in a golden balance. However, I do relish having a community of people with whom I can discuss the nature of the Divine, and with whom to explore how mere mortals can conceptualize that which lies far beyond the limits of our walnut brain. I struggle to understand, yet my failure to understand means nothing.

Gradually, age has strengthened my awe of a universe whose richness and complexity cannot be grasped. It feels good to give thanks for all that is part of my life, very little of which is the fruit of my own efforts. I have started thinking of religion not in its strictest sense, dividing people into narrow, and often opposing camps, but in its noblest sense, as a guide to ethical behavior.

> Donniel Hartman ... argues heretically that the great
> monotheistic religions are fatally flawed — by an obses-
> sive focus on God that overwhelms ... doing what is just
> and right. ... To be a Jew is to see other people, and to feel
> responsible to their needs. ... When the potential convert
> comes to Hillel, asking that he teach him the whole Torah, ...

Hillel doesn't even mention God. Hillel says, "What's hateful to you, do not do unto others. That's the whole Torah." [12]

I have learned a great deal about Judaism and about other religions since taking a few tentative steps as part of my transition to retirement. I have learned that how I act and what I do matters far more than what I believe or don't believe. I have learned that every human is a spark of the Divine, which is why we feel that warm glow whenever we are helpful in some small way to another person or to another creature. What matters is how we care for one another. To the age-old question "Am I my brother's keeper?" Judaism and other religions reply with a hearty "Yes, indeed! You are also your sister's keeper, and the keeper of the stranger whom you must welcome into your home and onto your land. Never forget that you were once strangers enslaved in Egypt. You have fled from drought, famine, autocratic pharaohs, and from injustice itself. You know what it means to suffer."

Stories are never absolute; they are metaphors that invite us to ask questions. Stories help us expand our awareness as we explore more deeply. Every culture and every religion seeks ways to understand the beginning of The Beginning. Every culture has its tricksters and snakes that allow us to explore evil and how to counteract it.

Humans tell stories in order to make sense of a universe beyond comprehension. Sacred books are one way to explore human nature and the extent of human responsibilities. Around the globe, scriptures and oral traditions are filled with images that allow us to understand. A snake extending an apple to a woman in a garden, this we can conceptualize, but Evil? How shall we picture a concept so vague, varied, and elusive?

One particular set of stories is my heritage. Others have theirs. Tales of frog and whale, or of Shiva and Shakti, these are no less valid an avenue of exploration than are my stories of Joseph and his brothers, or of Moses descending Sinai to bring down the Ten Commandments. What matters is how we understand those commandments, and whether we live accordingly. If it says "Do not kill," must we scrap soldiering and dissolve the military complex? Must we become pacifists and let a few psychopaths run the world? Does slaughtering animals count as killing?

I take nothing literally, and I do not view biblical events as historically accurate. Still, I acknowledge the need for starting points. I rejoice when someone says that Abraham and Sarah were ancestors who demonstrated that God dwells in the human heart, and that God is made manifest when we show kindness to others.

I have come to believe that my individual existence matters, that my life has value and meaning, and that I've been placed on earth for some purpose, even if its exact nature is unclear to me.

To explore such questions, it helps to have a community of people interested in reading and discussing the same stories. It helps to set aside special times to leave behind the world of working and doing, and to spend that time going inward, which is how I define prayer. I need a time not just to ask for what I want, but to open myself to ever broader possibilities of awareness. A time to grow in spirit, so that I will have the strength and courage to deal with the world and its problems.

As my experience and that of other elders demonstrates, we should not shy away from asking big questions. Why was I born? Does God exist? If so, in what form? Is one religion right and all others wrong? Are atheists right? Is everything a matter of belief? One may not find answers, but the questions are an important adjunct to aging.

For these reasons and more, I invite you to let go of thinking that you must always know the answer. Instead, let us welcome the opportunity to speculate, to wonder if ... or whether just possibly ... or whether perhaps ...

Let us welcome the questions, and join a great poet in patient speculation:

> I beg you to have patience with everything unresolved in
> your heart and try to love the questions themselves as if
> they were locked rooms or books written in a very foreign

language. Don't search for the answers, which could not be given to you now, because you would not be able to live them. And the point is to live everything. Live the questions now. Perhaps, someday in the future, you will gradually, without ever noticing it, live your way into the answer.[13]

—⁓—

IDEA:

Aging is the time to speculate, to wonder if our lives have meaning and purpose, or whether we are just here for the blink of an eye and owe nothing to the Universe.

ACTION:

Reflect upon whether or not you agree:

- *Life is the story; death is only punctuation.*[14]

- I draw comfort from my faith, not faith in the God of happy endings for good people ... but the faith that life is not meaningless just because it is not endless.[15]

- I *do not believe that either Heaven or Hell await.* Both, to me, are human projections, the former as the culmination of every conceivable desire, the latter as the ultimate in human fear and paranoia. What I expect is some unconceptualized reality that confounds my small brain, as does the magnitude, magnificence, and complexity of the universe.

- If I am indeed my brother's keeper, how can I turn my back on the suffering of others? Does the complexity of the issue absolve me of my ultimate responsibility?

Deeper Still

Feeling Gratitude

We must each lead a way of life with self-awareness and compassion, and do as much as we can. Then, whatever happens, we will have no regrets.

— Emily Lyman

Poet Emily Lyman writes:

I am thoughtful and poetic.
I wonder about everything that I see
why it snakes through my head instead of passing by
like a cloud.
I hear the thrum of thoughts ... like raindrops on the
roof.

Like Emily, I have days when thoughts snake endlessly through my head, refusing to be silent, ceaselessly thrumming, and as dismal as the winter rain rapping on the roof. Days when I start to fear that humans are hopeless, selfish, incorrigibly self-centered creatures, too lazy/ignorant/unevolved to aspire to a world of peace. I start to fear that humans will never learn to share harmoniously or to divide fairly this precious planet and its treasures — clean air and water, nourishing food, along with the finest products of human endeavour. And yet, as the first line of Emily's poem compels me to acknowledge, no matter how gloomy my thoughts, they are inseparable from my identity. I do wonder about so much, a trait that makes me thoughtful even if I lack Emily's poetic touch.

In the forword to the poet's slender volume, Emily's mother wrote these words:

> Emily fought leukemia for the majority of her life. She had been cancer-free for five years when the leukemia returned. We were in complete shock. I remember bursting into tears and looking over at Emily only to see a stoic face filled with determination and a wish to understand the facts. She asked if she was going to die and all I could answer was that her life would be shorter than most.
>
> Emily died 42 hours later. In her final moments, she understood what was happening in her body even before we did. She took control of the situation and suddenly declared:
>
>> Say goodbye to my friends.
>> Make sure my Secret Santa gets his gift.
>> Please do something to make me famous.
>> I'm done.
>
> That was it. She lay down, fell asleep, never to awaken. Emily was fifteen.[1]

Each time I think of young Emily, I become freshly aware of the gift of life that I have been granted. I have already been privileged to live eighty years. God willing, I shall live another fifteen, the equivalent of an entire lifetime for Emily. How shall I not be grateful for every day granted to me, even if, occasionally, it is a day of endless rain?

Sometimes, I try to imagine what Theodore Roszack calls "the view from the hospital bed." How it will be when I am in that bed, uncertain whether I will ever leave it alive.

> Then, if you have enough stamina and presence of mind, you find yourself saying "If I ever get out of here, I'm going to remember every moment of this life like a catechism

lesson. Something so simple that everybody ought to know it. But they don't. If you're alive, if you're on your own feet, if you're out of pain ... be thankful! For every little thing, because none of the "little" things are really little. Having a meal, looking out the window, feeding Gregory the blue jay his daily peanut, giving Henry the cat a friendly rub, taking a walk, reading a good book. ... Above all, just being with people you love, if only to make small talk, if only to feel their caring nearness and know you exist in somebody's respectful awareness. Remember how these things looked from the hospital bed, when you felt broken into a hundred, scattered, irreparable pieces, when there was a good chance it might all be taken away from you once and for all. Remember how rare, special, marvelous — how sufficient.[2]

Those of us who are lucky enough to be elders have been given a second chance. A chance to appreciate at a deeper level. A chance to reach out. Not a chance to fix it all, for that is beyond any individual's powers, but a chance to do some small thing to tip the scales of life toward the Good.

Adding an ounce of goodness can become a daily habit. I have tried for many years to follow that principle, and to do so in ever-expanding circles. I seek to do one thing for family, one for a friend, one for others, hoping my small stone dropped into a pond will radiate outward. For family and friends, that act may be a hug, a phone call, an email, or a card or note. For the next circle, it may be as simple as smiling at a stranger or picking up litter.

Stephanie Dowrick writes:

Each time I choose the more loving direction, ... kinder impulse, ... most encouraging word; each time I choose to silence my complaint, my criticism, or to deal with a conflict non-violently; each time I ... more wholeheartedly ...

appreciate or express gratitude for what is around me; each time I offer help or comfort selflessly, or pause to reflect, give inner thanks or praise, or align myself freshly with my finest impulses and self, I rediscover the source of my spiritual life — and I live it.[3]

Perhaps it is the fact that so many elders are spending time and energy bringing drops of kindness to the world that contributes to the glow that characterizes this new cohort of active elders. David Brooks notes that we become what we repeatedly practice:

Character is built in the course of your inner confrontation. Character is a set of dispositions, desires, and habits that are slowly engraved during the struggle against your own weakness. You become more disciplined, considerate, and loving through a thousand small acts of self-control, sharing, service, friendship, and refined enjoyment.[4]

Recently I attended a conference marking the fiftieth anniversary of *Nostra Aetate*. Perhaps for you as it was for me, the term is unfamiliar. *Nostra Aetate* was a declaration by the Second Vatican Council in 1965 that all people are created in the image of God. It also declared that the blame for Jesus' death may no longer be laid at the door of Jews who lived over two thousand years ago, let alone blamed upon the Jews who are alive today. Furthermore, it urged Catholics and Muslims especially to forget the Crusades and the hostilities of the past in order to work together today.

While some disagreement followed the use of "forget" — historians in the wake of Toynbee remind us that those who forget the past are likely, even condemned to repeat it in some form — it was fascinating to see priests and rabbis and imams gathered at the same conference table to discuss mutual understanding. One speaker quoted Heraclitus: "No man ever steps into the same river twice, for it's not the same river and he's not the same person." Similarly, I'd wager that not one of the hundreds of people in attendance left the same as when he/she arrived that morning. The animated conversations I overheard in the lobby demonstrated the change that each participant had undergone.

I attended in an effort to weather my own storm. Just before the conference, I had spoken with a young man studying at an American university. One Saturday evening at a campus pizza party, he mentioned that he was Jewish. Immediately, a classmate reached out a hand and asked to feel his horns. My young friend was shocked. I was less surprised, but equally troubled that this ancient superstition — that Jews are the spawn of the devil and thus sprout horns — has not vanished along with the Middle Ages. My experience has been that accusations against the Jews do not vanish; they merely change form. While Jews are no longer accused of poisoning wells and bringing on the plague, references to Jews controlling the banks has shifted from 1930s Germany to contemporary Wall Street, with "control of the media" thrown in for good measure.

Religion has long been the most universal, and in some ways, the most problematic of groupings in terms of fostering hatreds. Nations are a close second, but their alliances fluctuate more frequently. Former enemies become friends, as did France and Germany, while former allies like America and Russia become opponents vying for supremacy.

I believe that it is possible to overcome fear of the other, and the ubiquitous distrust of all that is different. That distrust may well be deeply rooted within the human psyche, dating back to prehistoric times when all that was unknown may indeed have been dangerous, whether it was an untested berry growing on a bush, a never-before-seen animal emerging from cave, or a human figure crouching in the jungle. If, given today's technology, we fail to overcome that primal fear, that urge to strike out before we can be struck, then we risk destroying everything.

Opening up our hearts and minds, adding an ounce of goodness to the scales, weathering our personal storms without allowing hatred or bitterness to color our response, these are what elders can and must do with the gift of time.

All elders should use this gift well. We should feel the warmth and softness of a child's hand. Savor the soothing coolness of a glass of water. Touch someone. Listen. Allow our senses to fill the present moment. Show kindness and thoughtfulness. Smile to brighten someone's day.

Age gives us the second chance not granted to Emily Lyman who reached out to so many people during her short life. Let us use our extra years as best we can. Let us imagine that view from the hospital bed. May it lead us to appreciate what is good, and may it lead us to do our utmost to leave this world in slightly better shape at our death than was the case at our birth. Then, as young Emily said, "whatever happens, we will have no regrets."

—⁓—

Having No Regrets

If I can stop one Heart from breaking
I shall not live in vain
If I can ease one Life the Aching
Or cool one pain
Or help one fainting Robin
Unto his Nest again
I shall not live in Vain.

— Emily Dickinson

RECENTLY, I LISTENED AT LENGTH TO A FRIEND who berated himself for all the ways he had failed. Although he had done well by the usual measures of success, he could not forgive himself for not having done better, especially where his family is concerned. Elements of dysfunctionality that he now saw passed on from his children to his grandchildren consumed his every waking moment.

Although I reminded him of the ways in which he had repeatedly demonstrated good judgment, nothing I said could lift him from the well of guilt into which he had lowered himself.

He freely acknowledged that the parenting he received had left much to be desired. He accepted that his parents had been shaped by attitudes prevalent in the world of their youth, but he could not extend the same forgiveness to himself.

I thought of this friend when I stumbled upon a delightful little book with the intriguing title *Fail, Fail Again, Fail Better* by the Buddhist nun Pema Chödrön. She advises learning to "welcome the unwelcome" rather than blame other people, other circumstances, or even ourselves for all the unexpected developments in every life.[5]

I thought of this friend again when I was invited to formulate an "ethical will" — words of wisdom that I was to set down for my children and grandchildren. I declined the invitation. Doing so would place too much power in my hands. Besides, I do not want my loved ones ever to think that they have failed to live up to my expectations. My loved ones are fine people who will make mistakes, as will we all. Like everyone, they must forge their own life, fashioning it as they see fit. I cannot claim to know which is the right path for them, and I certainly don't wish to be a disembodied voice speaking from beyond the grave, wagging my finger at their mistakes. They must do as I have done: attempt, for better or worse, to the best of their judgment, to live their own life as best they can.

I thought of this reluctance to puff myself up as an all-knowing elder when I found myself updating my actual will, a periodic necessity that inevitably causes me to rethink who and what really matters. This time, I was asked about my wishes if the unthinkable were to happen. How would I dispose of my worldly goods if my entire family were to be wiped out in a single disaster?

It is a question for which I found myself completely unprepared. I know that such disasters happen, but I tell myself that they will continue to happen only in faraway places. In like fashion, I tell myself that humans will surely wake up and step back from the brink of mutual destruction, or worse, the inconceivable end of planet earth. I so desperately want life to continue beyond my demise.

Physician Atul Gawande has observed that the nearer we approach the end of our days, the greater our need for something more than mere individualism and self-interest.

> If self-interest were the primary source of meaning in life, then it wouldn't matter to people if an hour after their death everyone they know were to be wiped from the face of the earth. Yet it matters greatly to most people. We feel that such an occurrence would make our lives

meaningless. The only way death is not meaningless is to see yourself as part of something greater: a family, a community, a society. If you don't, mortality is only a horror.[6]

Family has lain at the core of meaningful existence since the evolution of human life. Those who find themselves bereft of family often suffer greatly. On holidays especially, as I gaze about the table at my real and my "adoptive" family, I remember my father who had to leave parents, brothers, sisters, nieces, nephews, and cousins behind in order to save his wife and child. I spare a thought for him and for everyone who aches with loneliness.

In the absence of family, or perhaps in addition to it, belonging to a community becomes more important as we age. When the companionship of workmates fades into history, new sources of "togetherness" become imperative. Some people find community on the basis of religious affiliation; others discover it through shared creativity. Most people in my world find community through social activism. They work for change, be it political, environmental, egalitarian, or in pursuit of a more loving and peaceful world.

Belonging to some form of group may well be as indispensable as water is to a fish. Family, community, society — Gawande is absolutely right in saying that all of us require "devotion to something more than ourselves" for our lives to be endurable and meaningful.

My thoughts here fly to Frank, who is suffering from an incurable neurological condition. He cannot be part of a community in a formal sense, and not long ago, he investigated the possibility of voluntarily terminating his life while he was still physically capable of doing so. Something clearly led him to change his mind, at least for now. Despite pain and physical limitations, he has decided to write about the dying process, and how it unfolds for him. Even on his death bed, Frank cares. He is seeking a way to make his life meaningful.

As the years pass, most people seek some sense of purpose. We'd like life to continue beyond our death, and deep down, often unvoiced,

dwells the secret hope that our own small lives will have made a difference. While attending a solemn ceremony in the BC Legislature, I
noted these words inscribed upon the wall of the rotunda:

> I am driven by a deep passion and need to make a dif-
> ference and leave this world a little better than when I
> arrived. That's what keeps me going.
> — Rick Hansen, CC, OBC.

Even elders who can reflect back on a lifetime of achievement or
upon a family well-launched, find that their task has not yet been
completed, and that their search is not yet at an end. The past often
fails to be enough.

Karen Armstrong captures the thrust of this enduring search:

> We are meaning-seeking creatures and we fall very easily
> into despair if we fail to make sense of our lives. We find
> the prospect of our inevitable extinction hard to bear ...
> We find it astonishing that we are here at all and want to
> know why.[7]

The search for meaning, universal among humans, is no easy
undertaking. Armstrong's "why" puts us squarely in front of the Great
Mysteries of Life, for which there is no ready explanation.

Viktor Frankl, who confronted death on a daily basis in Auschwitz,
understood this predicament. He concluded that "what matters ... is
not the meaning of life in general but rather the specific meaning of a
person's life at a given moment."[8]

Ben-Shahar, creator of the most popular course in Harvard's history, puts it this way:

> Having a purpose, a goal that provides a sense of direc-
> tion, imbues our individual actions with meaning, and
> from experiencing life as a collection of disjointed pieces,
> we begin to experience it as a masterpiece.[9]

Those disjointed pieces may come from the pursuit of a singular goal. I have a friend who is celebrating fifty years as a member of his local chapter of the International Lions Club, a chapter he was instrumental in founding. I cannot lay claim to such consistency. Instead, I thrive on variety and fresh challenge. In the past fifty years, I have marched for civil rights, for peace, for Indigenous rights, for the environment, for murdered sex-trade workers. I have helped shelter draft-dodgers, abused women, homeless animals. I have sat on and chaired more committees than I can remember. I have fund-raised for countless causes, at home and abroad.

Whether we throw our entire energy into one great project or into a multitude of causes matters less than that we go beyond thinking only of ourselves and of our creature comforts. Only by weaving together the strands of self, family, community, and society can we even contemplate making our last will and testament. Only then does it become possible to face death with a measure of equanimity.

—⁓—

Facing Death with Equanimity

Sleep is a death; oh make me try
By sleeping what it is to die,
And as gently lay my head
On my grave as now my bed.

— Thomas Browne

A LTHOUGH WE MIGHT CHOOSE TO TALK OF OTHER THINGS, from time to time my thoughts, and probably yours, turn to "end-of-life" concerns. Will I be able to manage a motorized scooter and roll to a park in the afternoon sunshine? Will someone fetch me in my wheelchair and take me to the occasional concert? Will I be gracious when an attendant spoons soup into my mouth?

Meanwhile, we make our wills, write up powers of attorney, prepare health care and funeral directives, and try to put our house in order.

For some elders, thinking about the end is helpful and calming. Here's how Mary Karr explains her attraction to T. S. Eliot's *The Waste Land:*

> Why read something so darkly despairing? The poem acts
> for me as a sort of vaccine against the horror it describes
> by injecting a nonlethal dosage of it.[10]

Rather than vaccinate themselves and practice acceptance, some people opt for denial or wishful thinking. I have a ski buddy who plays on a seniors' hockey team. His dream has long been to exit life either by hitting the boards or by colliding with a tree. I hope this will be his good fortune, but I fear that it may not.

Such denial can sometimes have baneful consequences. Recently, I heard that two acquaintances had been stricken with cancer. The prognosis was bad for both. One man continued as before, living in total denial of his disease and cheerfully pretending to family and friends that he'd soon be back to normal. To this day, his family is unsettled. Like his friends, they resent the fact that he never trusted them enough to speak openly and honestly. They cannot shake a lingering anger mingled with guilt over the fact that they never expressed their love for him. They feel deprived of a last meaningful "farewell."

The other man decided where and when he'd like to die, in his case "on the old sod," where he spent his remaining days researching family roots. He longed to come to terms with the cultural forces and family connections that had shaped his life. To those whom he expected never to see again, he bid adieu in a way that continues to enrich and inspire their lives.

A close friend has taken a different tack. She has adapted to needing round-the-clock care by welcoming each and every person who comes to her aid. Without exception, these are women from foreign lands. My friend expresses gratitude for their kindness, and she shows sincere interest in their past history and current struggles. "My own little United Nations," she fondly calls the multi-ethnic caregivers whose help has become essential.

Like this gracious woman, many of us will experience a lengthy period of decline and dependency. We can only hope that it will be counterbalanced in other ways. For most of us, this means a soothing touch and the presence of loved ones.

Recently, another friend honored me in a particular way. First, she entrusted me and a select few others with the knowledge that she had freely made the decision to end her life legally. It would happen with medical assistance on a preselected date. As the day came closer, she made time for me to pay one last visit. On that occasion, the words I had failed to formulate in advance simply issued from my mouth.

They seemed to match perfectly what she needed to hear. I will treasure those brief moments forever, along with the final silent kiss we exchanged.

This experience put me in mind of *The Farewell Party*, an Israeli film that, in a humorous way, makes a strong and rational case for assisted suicide when all that lies ahead is acute suffering and intubation. If we can go to the moon, surely we can offer choices about death, while ensuring that mass slaughter of the elderly and disabled is not a future reality!

Certainly, I can envisage the worst, when a political leader somewhere will promise huge tax savings the moment we "stop wasting money on ____." Already, some of our physicians are feeling conflicted and overwhelmed. At the same time, my optimism tells me that we are in good hands, and that neither doctors nor judges nor lawmakers nor the broader public will countenance anything but the most rigorous guidelines for end-of-life choices.

I also recognize that for some people, no matter what their earlier intentions, the will to live proves too strong. Over a period of years, my friend Lorelei collected every pill and medication prescribed by her doctor, plus bottles of over-the-counter sleeping pills. For years, she told her closest friends that she never wanted to be a burden on her children. Long after she became housebound, long after she became totally dependent on her children and on the caregivers who came to dress, bathe, and feed her, Lorelei talked about those pills. After her death, we found them unopened in her bedside drawer.

Circumstances have placed me among those who have had no direct experience of dependency, and only limited exposure to death in my immediate family. I never knew my grandparents or members of the extended family. They perished at the hands of the Nazis. I didn't really experience the death of my father which occurred the year I was away studying in Paris. It was lung cancer, but my parents didn't want to spoil my year abroad. Instead, in chatty airmail letters pre-signed by my father, my mother kept up the pretense that all was well. When the telegram arrived to summon me home, it was already too late.

Despite everything, my mother remained aware of small pleasures to her dying day. She seemed happier in her final years and seemed to bask in the sunshine of simply being alive.

In a letter to a friend, she wrote:

> I always think to keep busy, have friends, see friends, and get out of life just little things. If I can meet a friend, just go to the market with her, talk a little and go home again. I knit, I read a lot, bake for Helen and the girls, invite once in a while somebody for lunch or a cup of coffee, go for walks with my dog, simple things, and it makes me so happy. Never mind, I have my bad days too, but you get out of life what you put in.

I cannot read the words without longing to hear again her accented English and her European turn of phrase. When she died, it was peaceful. Resting comfortably in her armchair, a beloved granddaughter to one side, and me at the other, she breathed her last as we each gently stroked an arm and held her hand.

The loss was ours to bear, not hers. She was at rest. Just as a sentence is not finished until it has a full stop, so every life needs a dying to complete it. Hers was a death as gentle as her nature. Perhaps sometimes death does receive us as the river receives a swan:

> This laboring of ours with all that remains undone,
> as if still bound to it,
> is like the lumbering gait of the swan.
>
> And then our dying — releasing ourselves
> from the very ground on which we stood —
> is like the way he hesitantly lowers himself
>
> Into the water. It gently receives him,
> and, gladly yielding, flows back beneath him,

as wave follows wave,
while he, now wholly serene and sure,
with regal composure,
allows himself to glide.[11]

When my daughter Reda undertook her rotation as a nurse in palliative care, she was struck by the stark contrast in how her patients encountered death. Some drifted away as gently as Rilke's swan. Others seemed locked in a desperate battle with a larger-than-life demonic figure whose stranglehold left them gasping for breath. They died angry and exhausted by a fight they could not win.

I have no desire to be consumed by anger during my last moments on earth. I do not wish to engage in a deadly struggle so that I may breathe a few days longer. I'd rather end my days watching a beautiful sunset or gazing at flowers in a garden. I'd rather die while feeling the tender touch of a loved one. Those Swiss clinics have the right idea. When the time comes, chocolate will be distributed to everyone, to the patient who has chosen assisted death over further suffering, and to those whose presence is their last gift to a loved one. Chocolate to ensure that the last taste of life will be sweet.

Yielding to the Inevitable

It's all a mystery, so much is mysterious.
And we are here to experience it.
And in the How, there lies the whole difference.

— Hugo von Hofmannsthal

I N A SMALL TOWN IN GERMANY, an article in the local newspaper featured a photo of a centenarian against the backdrop of her beloved balcony garden. The article stated that she was expecting a visitor from Canada — the daughter of the Jewish family for whom she had worked before the war.

Tini was clearly pleased with my visit, and with the numerous other visitors, all of whom brought tortes, tarts, and sweet treats to feast upon, just barely leaving room for the two trays bearing 100 candles. Tini blew out all but four on the first tray, and all 50 on the second. Her lungs are clearly healthy even though she has been confined to her apartment since a fall on the ice three years ago. Still, neither she nor her family want anything to do with a nursing home (they claim these are dreadful places where you go only to die) and she wants to stay within her own four walls. Tini remains mentally alert and has retained her store of pithy sayings. She seems as comfortable with the reality of aging as she was when I first reconnected with her sixty years after I was torn from her arms by my panic-stricken parents as they fled the Nazi invaders. Tini was still a spry eighty-five at the time of our reconnection, and her favourite expression was "*Herrgott, ich bin bereit, aber es pressiert nicht!* (Lord, I'm ready, but if You are busy elsewhere, there's no need to rush!)"

Unlike those who hearken to the siren song of travel, adventure, and external exploration, Tini seems more inclined to go within. I have never seen a book or a magazine in her home, and her grandson told me that she refused his offer of a TV. Gradually, the outside world has stopped mattering.

Angeles Arrien claims that it is part of the aging process "to see our lives with new eyes so we can begin to prepare for the ultimate new experience, which is our death."[12]

To prepare for death, even to conceive of death as the next adventure, is new in Western thought. Often, we still dare not even speak the word. Instead of dying, our loved ones "pass" or "pass on" — but invariably either *peacefully* or after a *brave struggle* with illness. Jokes may be allowed, but even in religious circles, serious discussion of what may lie ahead is generally avoided.

Whence cometh our concept of death? As I child, I recall thinking of death as something that only happened to animals. Squawking chickens grew still when a long, sharp knife was thrust into their beak. Later, my mother would plunge them into a bath of hot water, and I would help pluck the feathers before she sliced open their rear end, and inserted her hand deeply into the cavity to pull out the heart, the liver, and the intestines in a single quivering mass.

Only later did I become aware that people, including children, could die. Over seventy years have passed, yet I still have nightmares of awakening to the sounds of panic-stricken adults shouting and dashing about the farmhouse. I tiptoed to the window where an enormous ball of flame lit up the night sky. A car on the adjacent highway had collided with a gasoline truck. The truck driver, two children and their parents died in the fiery crash that still haunts my nightmares.

Despite annual exposure to a Shakespearean tragedy in high school, I don't recall giving death much thought until university where I encountered Goethe's unforgettable poem *"Der Erlkönig."* The poem depicts the malevolent Scandinavian elf-king in the very act of snuffing out the life a child cradled in his father's arms. The poem captures brilliantly the clop of the horse's hooves as the Erlking gallops ever closer. Each time I read it, I shiver involuntarily, picturing the Erlking reaching out with icy fingers to snatch the soul of the innocent babe. This image morphed into my adult concept of death. Death as an irresistible figure, larger than life, galloping through the night to seize and to silence the human heart.

Only recently was that image of death dislodged from my imaginings. In a museum in Amsterdam, I stood transfixed before a Van Gogh painting. To my astonishment, he painted Death neither as the Grim Reaper nor as a menacing Horseman of the Apocalypse. Van Gogh paints Death as a small human figure with a scythe in his right hand. For a moment, he pauses in a field of golden grain.

I stood stunned, seeing death for the first time as insignificant, as completely dwarfed by the richness of life, for which the vast stretch of ripening golden grain is the perfect symbol. I have held on to that image of death as a small manikin who will one day come to cut me down, separating me from my roots with one swift blow of his sharp scythe. Meanwhile, I continue to see myself as that field of golden grain, feeling so fortunate to have had time to ripen and to enjoy being kissed by so much that constitutes the sunshine of life.

For others, and especially for those with no belief in an afterlife, giving serious thought to death can be unspeakably difficult. For them, death represents no more than the mechanical breakdown of the material body. For some, the breakdown will be anticipated as a surcease from pain and dependency; for others, it will be accompanied by grief at parting from loved ones.

The religiously inclined tend to see death as the gateway to another life. While some may fear a final judgment followed by hellfire and damnation, my intuition is that most people think of themselves not as dreadful sinners but rather as limited and ordinary humans who did their best. Consequently, they hope to be rewarded by spending eternity in Heaven, Paradise, or some form of Nirvana. Belief in an afterlife in some form has existed in every culture since time immemorial.[13]

Strangely, despite the scientific advances that have prompted many to forsake established religions, belief in an afterlife has grown. In large measure, this is a result of the many reports cataloguing Near-Death Experiences (NDEs). Medical progress means that people who have clinically died can now be revived. I have two close friends who experienced cardiac failure and had to be "shocked" back to life. Both call themselves atheists, yet like growing numbers of people in a similar situation, they reported experiencing a beautiful and welcoming place.

The hope that medical science will someday allow frozen bodies to be revived with memory and personality intact has led to a growing interest in cryonics (currently priced at $200,000 for whole-body preservation, with head-only preservation available for around $80,000). I have no desire to experience such immortality, but I am intrigued by the concept of preparing for death as a moment of supreme consciousness, a concept that is called "deathing."

Had I not had the good fortune to experience its polar opposite, I'd be inclined to dismiss such a concept. Here's how it happened. Like the women in countless novels and films, I expected to be shrieking with pain when my children were born. I am no heroine, but thanks to training in the Lamaze method of natural childbirth, that was not the case. What I recall is how steadily my husband mopped the sweat from my brow while I did the hardest physical labor of my life. However, thanks to mental preparedness and mastery of rhythmic breathing, I was able to experience a moment of transcendent connection. Giving birth was a moment of ecstasy and wholeness whose intensity defies words.

That moment of ecstasy underlies my fascination with deathing, a process of preparation for an event that may be the most sublime moment in a lifetime. Had I not had the good fortune to experience birthing as a supreme moment of feeling connection with all life, I might have instantly dismissed this concept.

If deathing promises a comparable moment, then I am eager to be fully conscious. Here's how Anya Foos-Graber explains the concept:

> Deathing bears the same relationship to mere death as prepared childbirth bears to conventional births. ... Dying does not have to be steeped in pain and difficulty. ... While the stages preceding the death moment may be painful, frustrating, and terrifying, the death moment itself is beautiful when prepared for and not resisted.[14]

Of course, physical differences are real, and "natural" childbirth is not appropriate for all. Like women everywhere, I am grateful for scientific progress, and for medical advances in particular. At the end of my days, I too may be begging for whatever drug will ease my pain. However, if there is even the remotest possibility of encountering Death, I'd like to be awake and alert and aware for what may be the incomparable moment of transition — death not as mere ending, but as the experience of a lifetime.

Although I may or may not have the opportunity to experience my own death, I know that death awaits. I know also that I have consciously chosen to throw in my lot with philosophers and spiritual masters who have proposed since time immemorial that there is more to life than meets the eye.

I have chosen to believe that life is purposeful in some way not clear to the human brain. I have also chosen to believe that my soul needed to feel all the grief along with all the outrage and all the deep caring that has been my life for the last eighty years. It has been a great life, and I like to think that it may be my reward for sacrifices made and for good behavior in some prior existence. I die, however, with many questions unresolved.

At this age and stage of my growth, I find it comforting to think that someday, in some way, I might just get another chance to right the world's wrongs. I'd love to be reborn with greater wisdom, insight, compassion. I'd love to think I may yet live to see more birds and butterflies, to learn about the vastness of the cosmos, and to under-stand the complexities of human nature. I may be over eighty, but there's so much more, and I haven't even begun to scratch the surface.

Out, out, brief candle? Not yet, I hope. And not forever, I pray.

Notes

Preface

i. Theodore Roszack, *The Making of an Elder Culture: Reflections on the Future of America's Most Audacious Generation* (Gabriola Island, BC: New Society Publishers, 2009) 8.

ii. Quoted in Roszack, 1.

iii. Mark Nepo, *Facing the Lion, Being the Lion* (San Francisco: Conari Press, 2007) 66.

iv. Nancy Ellen Abrams, *A God That Could Be Real: Spirituality, Science, and the Future of our Planet* (Boston: Beacon Press, 2015) 146–7.

v. Frans B.M. de Waal, *The Age of Empathy: Nature's Lessons for a Kinder Society* (New York: McClelland & Stewart, 2009).

vi. Dacher Keltner, Jason Marsh, and Jeremy Adam Smith, The *Compassionate Instinct: The Science of Human Goodness* (New York: W.W. Norton and Co., 2010) 22.

Diving In

1. Friedrich Nietzsche, *Beyond Good and Evil*, Chapter V, "On the Natural History of Morals," 189.

2. Ray Robertson, *Why Not?: 15 Reasons to Live* (Windsor, ON: Biblioasis, 2011) 34.

3. A. Leung et al., "Embodied Metaphors and Creative Acts," *Psychological Science* 23, 2012, 502–9.

4. Thomas Moore, *A Life at Work: The Joy of Discovering What You Were Born to Do* (New York: Random House, 2008) 133.

5. David Niven, *It's Not About the Shark: How to Solve Unsolvable Problems* (New York: St. Martin's Press, 2014) 145–6.

6. Ibid., 144.

7. Harold Kushner, *When All You've Ever Wanted Isn't Enough* (New York: Simon & Schuster, 1986) 20.

8. Blaise Pascal, *Oeuvres Complètes* (Paris: Bibliothèque de la Pléiade, Gallimard, 1954) 1138.

9. Mihaly Csikszentmihalyi, *The Evolving Self: A Psychology for the Third Millennium* (New York: HarperCollins, 1993) 33.

10. Ibid.

11. George and Sedena Cappannelli, *Do Not Go Quietly: A Guide to Living Consciously and Aging Wisely for People Who Weren't Born Yesterday* (California: Agape Media International, 2013) 178–9.

12. Michael Gurian, *The Wonder of Aging: A New Approach to Embracing Life After Fifty* (New York: Simon & Schuster, 2013) 255.

13. Robert Jingen Gunn, *Journeys into Emptiness: Dōgen, Merton, Jung and the Quest for Transformation* (New York, Paulist Press, 2000) 7.

14. Ibid.

15. In the original form of this proverb *(Hyt ys old Englysch sawe: A mayde schuld be seen, but not herd)*, it was specifically young women who were expected to keep quiet. See the fifteenth century collection of homilies called [John] *Mirk's Festial*, compiled by an Augustinian clergyman c. 1450. http://www.phrases.org.uk/meanings/

16. Harold G. Koenig, M.D., *Purpose and Power in Retirement: New Opportunities for Meaning and Significance* (Radnor, Penn: Templeton Foundation Press, 2002) 7–8.

17. Bill Gates Sr., *Showing Up for Life: Thoughts on the Gift of a Lifetime* (New York: Random House, 2009) 11.

18. Nele Neuhaus, *I Am Your Judge*, translation by Steven T. Murray (New York: St Martin's Press, 2015) 130.

19. Rainer Maria Rilke, *Das Stundenbuch: Vom Mönchischen Leben*, lines 5 and 6 of the untitled poem beginning "Ich liebe meines Wesens Dunkelstunden." Translation by author.

20. Christopher Logue's poem "Come to the Edge" from *New Numbers* (London: Cape, 1969) 65–6. It was originally written for a poster advertising an Apollinaire exhibition at the ICA, in 1961 or 1962, and was titled "Apollinaire Said"; Hence, it is often misattributed to Guillaume Apollinaire

21. Joan Chittister, *Following the Path: The Search for a Life of Passion, Purpose and Joy* (New York: Random House, 2012) 61–2.

22. George E. Vaillant, *Aging Well: Surprising Guideposts to a Happier Life from the Landmark Harvard Study of Adult Development* (New York: Little, Brown & Co., 2002) 61.

Detoxing

1. David Brooks, *The Social Animal: The Hidden Source of Love, Character, and Achievement* (New York: Random House, 2011) 347.

2. Judith Viorst, *Necessary Losses: The Loves, Illusions, Dependencies, and Impossible Expectations That All of Us Have to Give Up in Order to Grow* (New York: Simon & Schuster, 1986) 299.

3. James Hollis, *Finding Meaning in the Second Half of Life: How to Finally Grow Up* (New York: Penguin, 2005) 90.

4. Oliver Sacks, *Gratitude* (New York: Knopf, 2015) 10–11.

5. Michael Gurian, op.cit., 16.

6. Atul Gawande, *Being Mortal: Medicine and What Matters in the End* (Toronto: Doubleday Canada, 2014) 95.

7. A Hebrew word meaning "mother of a child's spouse." English has no specific word for the relationship between parents of married children.

8. Shakespeare, *As You Like It*. "All the world's a stage" monologue.

9. See, for example, Yuval Noah Harari, *Homo Deus: A Brief History of Tomorrow* (Toronto, Penguin Random House Canada Limited, 2015).

10. John Koblin, "How Much Do We Love TV? Let Us Count the Ways." *New York Times*, June 30, 2016.

11. Atul Gawande, op.cit., 95.

12. Michael Gurian, op.cit., 235.

13. Joan Chittister, op.cit., 58.

14. Cited in Chittister, op.cit., 59.

15. John T. Cacioppo and William Patrick, *Loneliness: Human Nature and the Need for Social Connection* (New York: W.W. Norton & Co., 2008) 12.

16. Emily Dickinson, "If I Can Stop One Heart from Breaking," *Collected poems of Emily Dickinson* (New York: Gramercy Books, 1982) 5.

17. Angeles Arrien, *The Second Half of Life: Opening the Eight Gates of Wisdom* [Winner of the 2007 Nautilus Award for Best Book on Aging], (Boulder CO: Sounds True, 2005) 30.

18. Jimmy Carter, *The Virtues of Aging* (New York: The Ballantine Publishing Group, 1998) 56.

19. Kevin Solomons, *Born to Be Worthless: The Power of Low Self-Esteem* (South Carolina: Independent Publishing Platform, 2013).

20. David Suzuki, personal communication sent via Deanna L. Bayne, Executive Assistant, July 19, 2016.

21. Viktor E. Frankl, *Man's Search for Meaning* (Boston: Beacon Press, 2006) 102.

22. Mason Currey, *Daily Rituals: How Artists Work* (New York: Knopf, 2013) 218.

23. Emily Esfahani-Smith, *The Power of Meaning: Crafting a Life That Matters* (Toronto: Viking, 2017) 78.

24. Carla Wintersgill, "A Life with Purpose Lasts Longer, Researchers Find," *Globe and Mail*, June 17, 2009.

25. Elkhonon Goldberg, *The Wisdom Paradox: How Your Mind Can Grow Stronger as Your Brain Grows Older* (New York: Penguin, 2005) 8.

26. Jimmy Carter, op.cit., 56.

27. Kristin Samuelson, "Close Friends Linked to a Sharper Memory: Maintaining Strong Social Networks Seems to Be Linked to Slower Cognitive Decline," *Northwestern Now*, November 1, 2017.

28. André Picard, "All the Lonely People," *The United Church Observer*, June 2016.

29. Martha Perkins, "Seniors Feel More Connected than Young People: Survey," *Vancouver Courier*, November 30, 2017.

Discovering

1. Alberto Manguel, *Curiosity* (New Haven: Yale University Press, 2015) 3.
2. Michel de Montaigne,"De l'Amitié." XXVIII, Translation Project Gutenberg's *The Essays of Montaigne, Complete.*
3. Martha Perkins op.cit.,
4. Lyndsay Green, *You Could Live a Long Time: Are You Ready?* (Toronto: Thomas Allen Publishers, 2010) 22.
5. Harold Kushner, *Living a Life That Matters* (New York: Random House, 2001) 116–9.
6. Ibid.
7. Emad Ahmed, "Why Have Men Become So Lonely — and How Does It Affect Their Health?" *New Statesman*, November 26, 2015.
8. Elizabeth Renzetti, "Life of Solitude: A Loneliness Crisis is Looming," *Globe and Mail*, September 18, 2015.
9. Hara Estroff Marano, "The Big Stall", *Psychology Today*, April 2016.
10. Cacioppo & Patrick, op.cit., 178–9.
11. Matthew Fox, *A Spirituality Named Compassion and the Healing of the Global Village, Humpty Dumpty and Us* (San Francisco: Harper & Row, 1979) 2–3.
12. Daniel Goleman, *Social Intelligence: The New Science of Human Relationships* (New York: Random House, 2006) 54.
13. Keltner, Marsh and Smith, op.cit., 13.
14. Jonathan Haidt, *The Righteous Mind: Why Good People Are Divided by Religion and Politics* (New York: Pantheon Books, 2012) 26.
15. Harold S. Kushner, *Nine Things I Have Learned About Life* (New York: Anchor Books, 2015) 80.
16. Gareth Cook, "The Moral Life of Babies," *Scientific American*, November 2013.
17. Anne Hines, *Parting Gifts* (Toronto: McArthur & Co., 2009) 167.

18. Deborah Serani, *Depression in Later Life: An Essential Guide* (Maryland: Rowman & Littlefield, 2016) 2.

19. Martin E.P. Seligman, *Authentic Happiness: Using the New Positive Psychology to Realize Your Potential for Lasting Fulfillment* (New York: Simon & Schuster, 2002).

20. Richard David Precht, *Who Am I? And If So, How Many?* (New York: Random House, 2011) 247–8.

21. Ibid.

22. Mark Nepo, op.cit., 30–1.

23. Sean Meshorer, *The Bliss Experiment: 28 Days to Personal Transformation* (New York: Simon & Schuster, 2012) 95.

24. Seligman, op.cit., 119.

25. Colin Beavan, *How to Be Alive: A Guide to the Kind of Happiness That Helps the World* (New York: HarperCollins, 2016) 43.

26. Peter Block, *The Answer to How Is Yes: Acting on What Matters* (San Francisco: Berrett-Koehler, 2002) 89–91.

Daring

1. Douglas Quan, "RCMP Looks Overseas to Stop Flow of Drugs. But How Reliable is China as a Partner in the Fight Against Fentanyl?" *National Post*, November 25, 2016.

2. See Irving Abella and Harold Troper, *None Is Too Many: Canada and the Jews of Europe, 1933–1948* (Toronto: Lester Publishing Ltd., 1983).

3. Alex Kershaw, *The Liberator* (New York: Random House, 2012) 281.

4. A soldier writing home to his wife about killing Jewish babies in Belarus. Quoted by Adam Gopnik, "Blood and Soil," *The New Yorker*, September 21, 2015.

5. Emily Dickinson, *The Laurel Poetry Series*, ed. Richard Wilbur (New York: Dell, 1960) 35.

6. Donna Tartt, *The Goldfinch* (New York: Little, Brown and Company, 2013) 767.

7. Frans de Waal, op.cit., 159.

8. "Canada Is Leading The Pack In Mixed Unions," *Macleans*, Editorial, July 29, 2014.

Delving Deeper

1. Ben Ehrenreich, "The Leveller: Famine in East Africa," *The London Review of Books*, Vol. 39, No. 16, August 17, 2017.

2. Joan Chittister, *The Gift of Years: Growing Older Gracefully* (New York: BlueBridge, 2008) 126.

3. Erik H. Erikson et al., *Vital Involvement in Old Age* (New York: W.W. Norton & Company, 1986) 334.

4. Speech delivered at UBC by Samantha Nutt, November 16, 2015.

5. Steven Chase, "Canada Now the Second Biggest Arms Exporter to Middle East, Data Show," *Globe and Mail*, updated July 12, 2016.

6. Kevin Solomons, op.cit., 77.

7. Stephanie Dowrick, *Choosing Happiness: Life and Soul Essentials* (New York, Penguin, 2005) 26.

8. Adam Gopnik, "The Illiberal Imagination," *New Yorker*, March 20, 2017.

9. Jonathan Sacks, *To Heal a Fractured World: The Ethics of Responsibility* (Montreal: McGill-Queens University Press, 2005) 261.

10. "Gravitational Waves Detected, Confirming Einstein's Theory," *New York Times*, February 12, 2016.

11. Albert Einstein, "The World As I See It."

12. David Horovitz, "God Must Not Be Our Top Priority," *The Times of Israel*, June 29, 2016.

13. Rainer Maria Rilke, *Letters to a Young Poet*: Translation M. D. Herter Norton (New York: W. W. Nortons and Company, 1993) 34–5

14. Harold S. Kushner, *Conquering Fear: Living Boldly in an Uncertain World* (New York: Alfred A. Knopf, 2009) 157.

15. Ibid, 156.

Deeper Still

1. Permission to quote these words graciously given by Emily's mother Monica Lyman in a personal communication, April 28, 2017.

2. Roszack, op.cit., 282.

3. Stephanie Dowrick *Seeking the Sacred: Transforming our View of Ourselves and One Another* (New York: Penguin, 2011) 9.

4. David Brooks, *The Road to Character* (New York: Random House, 2015) 263–4.

5. Pema Chödrön, *Fail, Fail Again, Fail Better: Wise Advice for Leaning into the Unknown* (Boulder, CO: Sounds True, 2015) 31.

6. Atul Gawande, op.cit., 126–7.

7. Karen Armstrong, *Fields of Blood: Religion and the History of Violence* (New York: Knopf, 2015) 6.

8. Viktor E. Frankl, op.cit., 101–2.

9. Tal Ben-Shahar, *Happier* (New York: McGraw-Hill, 2007) 40.

10. Mary Karr. Introduction. *The Waste Land and Other Writings*, T.S.Eliot (New York: Modern Library Classics, 2001).

11. Rainer Maria Rilke, "The Swan," translation by Joanna Macy and Anita Barrows.

12. Angeles Arrien, op.cit., 31.

13. Herbie Brennan, *Death: The Great Mystery of Life* (New York: Carroll & Graf, 2002) 126.

14. Anya Foos-Graber, *Deathing: An Intelligent Alternative for the Final Moments of Life* (Maine: Nicolas Hays Inc., 1989) 16–7.

Index

About the Author

HELEN WILKES, PH.D., is an energized octogenarian who survived a lifetime of hardships ranging from fleeing Nazi Germany as a child to navigating personal and professional obstacles as an adult. She persevered and created a richly rewarding life. Retirement has been the icing on her cake, bringing inner transformation and freedom. Helen is author of the award-winning book *Letters from the Lost*. She lives in Vancouver, Canada.

A Note about the Publisher

New Society Publishers is an activist, solutions-oriented publisher focused on publishing books for a world of change. Our books offer tips, tools, and insights from leading experts in sustainable building, homesteading, climate change, environment, conscientious commerce, renewable energy, and more — positive solutions for troubled times.

We're proud to hold to the highest environmental and social standards of any publisher in North America. This is why some of our books might cost a little more. We think it's worth it!

- We print all our books in North America, never overseas
- All our books are printed on **100% post-consumer recycled paper,** processed chlorine free, with low-VOC vegetable-based inks (since 2002)
- Our corporate structure is an innovative employee shareholder agreement, so we're one-third employee-owned (since 2015)
- We're carbon-neutral (since 2006)
- We're certified as a B Corporation (since 2016)

At New Society Publishers, we care deeply about *what* we publish — but also about *how* we do business.

Download our catalog at https://newsociety.com/Our-Catalog or for a printed copy please email info@newsocietypub.com or call 1-800-567-6772 ext 111

New Society Publishers
ENVIRONMENTAL BENEFITS STATEMENT

For every 5,000 books printed, New Society saves the following resources:[1]

22	Trees
1,976	Pounds of Solid Waste
2,174	Gallons of Water
2,836	Kilowatt Hours of Electricity
3,592	Pounds of Greenhouse Gases
15	Pounds of HAPs, VOCs, and AOX Combined
5	Cubic Yards of Landfill Space

[1]Environmental benefits are calculated based on research done by the Environmental Defense Fund and other members of the Paper Task Force who study the environmental impacts of the paper industry.

MIX
Paper from
responsible sources
FSC® C016245
www.fsc.org

new society
PUBLISHERS
www.newsociety.com